Google Apps Express

The Fast Way to Start Working in the Cloud

by James Beswick

About the Author

James Beswick is an award-winning writer who has appeared in various technology magazines and blogs. He has a B.Sc. in Management and Computer Science from Royal Holloway College, University of London and is also Google Analytics IQ Certified.

He has worked for a variety of Fortune 500 companies in online project and product management, specializing in implementing web-based technologies to help organizations to maximize their revenue opportunities online. James also provides webinars and seminars to help SMEs get the most out of Internet-based technology.

Also by this author:

- *"Getting Productive With Google Apps"* (January 2009)
- *"Ranking Number One: 50 Essential Tips to Boost Your Search Engine Results"* (June 2010)

Acknowledgments

This book would not exist without the teams of engineers at the Googleplex whose Internet revolution is just beginning – I avidly follow their developments and admire their dedication to pushing the bounds of what is possible and practical. And thanks to everyone in the Google Apps community for continuously improving this platform.

Thanks to my family for their support.

Contact the author

Writing a book is no small task, and I'm always interested to hear about your success stories and feedback.

Please email james@oneuproar.com with your questions, comments and errata.

Visit **http://www.googtips.com** for additional content and resources.

Contents

1. Introduction

Google Apps is a comprehensive suite of applications built upon the technically sophisticated Google infrastructure. Yet despite the complexity behind the scenes, the speed and simplicity of using the products sets it apart from its desktop counterparts. There are millions of Google Apps users in the world, but this is a small number compared to how many businesses, groups or organizations could substantially improve their productivity and reduce costs by using the platform.

This book is about 'trying it out' which, by the way, is about as informal as it gets when looking at technology, but it's a core idea at Google. Their engineers basically look at problems, take user suggestions, and try a range of different approaches to see what works. The ones that aren't so great get retired (remember Google Lively?), the ones before their time are semi-retired (Google Wave), and the hugely successful ones become production-ready products, such as Google Apps. This is why so many Google products are described as beta – unlike traditional software, they're continually refined and improved while in a production environment.

Obviously the beta approach isn't the most popular in corporate IT departments, and is certainly not a concept fully-embraced by many in the technology community, though it's central to the Google method. The benefit of taking this informal approach is that it leads to iterative improvement, so that rather than building the final product from scratch based upon a prediction of what a customer wants, you build something that roughly approximates it, and then refine the product based upon user feedback.

The great part is that you can see how well Google Apps works for you without cutting any checks, setting aside any hardware, or really spending very much time at all. It's a great opportunity to see how good a fit this platform will be for your organization before you make any sort of commitment. Consequently, I've written this book for the entrepreneur who wants to get Google Apps working in the fastest way possible. As we delve into the different parts of the suite, you can sign up for services – for free – and test-drive each application to see if it will improve how you currently do things. You also have the choice of using as much or as little of the Google Apps suite as you need, as we'll see in subsequent chapters.

Unlike many technical guides, I don't investigate every feature and button extensively. There are several reasons for this, the main one being that Google Apps software changes regularly, rendering any attempt to document it outdated fairly quickly, and also there are many useful and undocumented features which warrant more explanation than the simple ones. Rather than describe each part slavishly (details of which can be found in Google's excellent online help), I've focused on the less obvious tips and tricks that often take a few months to discover. Also, since I can't predict how you intend to use this software, I've created fictional scenarios that illustrate possible use-cases. And from my experience in helping companies deploy Google Apps, I've included *Frequently Asked Questions* in every chapter to cover some of the issues that tend to reappear over and over.

Much of the journey here involves rolling up your sleeves and trying things out – don't worry, you can't really break anything, but you can discover new and interesting ways of being more productive. This technology is founded on a relatively new paradigm where there's no installed software on your machine, and collaboration and teamwork are as important as the work itself.

In terms of getting Google Apps into your organization, you may find that one of the great challenges is social rather than technical. Trying to spur users into experimenting with new tools can be a challenge, and there's is a natural reluctance (and arguably healthy skepticism) to new technology when the old technology seems to work just fine. But I think this time it's different. Google Apps is used by a growing number of individuals, companies, school groups, universities, church groups, Fortune 500s and start-ups. It is based upon a new way of looking at software, at group collaboration and the Internet.

In the next 10 chapters, I want to show you that not only will Google Apps save time and money, but the new model is nothing short of a revolution in the way we use software. Looking back in a few years, it will be clear that this was the starting point for a major change in software development and usage, and most major companies producing applications will trend in the same direction. So apart from getting in at the ground floor of this revolution, more importantly, it may well just be the most exciting upgrade you ever perform, and the first time your colleagues have used software that truly helps you work together.

GOOGLE APPS SUCCESS STORIES

At first, just a handful of employees at Sanmina-SCI began using Google Apps for tasks like e-mail, document creation, and appointment scheduling. Now, just six months later, almost 1,000 employees of the electronics manufacturing company go online to use Google Apps in place of the comparable Microsoft tools. "We have project teams working on a global basis and to help them collaborate effectively, we use Google Apps," says Manesh Patel, chief information officer of Sanmina-SCI, a company with $10.7 billion in annual revenue.

http://www.businessweek.com/print/technology/content/aug2008/tc2008082_445669.htm

The Old World of Office Software

One of the reasons I'm such a proponent of Google Apps is that it solves so many of the labor-intensive and frankly strange problems of the old world of office desktop software. Looking at where we've come from, and seeing the flaws with those technology models helps explain why we're heading into these new waters.

The Unconnected PC

Back when we all first started using PCs, the machines weren't connected to any form of network. Using the classic IBM PC-compatible, with Microsoft Windows and Microsoft Office, it worked reasonably well for a decade or so, especially since computers were only friendly to people with Computer Science degrees before these three major pieces came together.

Microsoft Windows introduced to the average non-technical user the concept of multi-tasking by having applications running in windows stacked on top of each other, and Office centralized many of the business-centric tasks in a handful of applications which these days almost every company in the world uses.

Users were comfortable creating data files, printing documents, taking those to meetings and feeling a substantial sense of progression from the typewriter. Then, when people wanted to share documents with each other – giving secretaries notes, sending spreadsheets to accountants, asking colleagues for help – file transfer emerged.

The Local Area Network

For quite a while, the floppy disk was king, allowing files to be moved from one isolated machine to another, until the Local Area Network (LAN) became popular. At this point, instead of transferring files physically, a file server was introduced in the middle where all the documents were stored, and certain shared devices such as laser printers and scanners were also placed on the network. As a method of sharing files, the floppy disk bowed to the local network.

This model also defined an era, and users became accustomed to sharing files with their coworkers in the same office and department. This led to a new problem: compatibility. The folks in marketing were using Apple Macs while accounting used Windows PCs and some colleagues had different versions of Microsoft Office. Worse still, as email flourished, there was no guarantee that a client or vendor or anyone else outside the organization could read the attachments, so the model naturally evolved again.

In this phase, the proprietary file formats of each application started to become highly problematic because you have no idea what systems other people used. Missing fonts and different versions gave rise to the creation of the Portable Document Format (PDF, created by Adobe in 1993). PDF at least guaranteed every user had the same view of a document regardless of which platform or application generated it, though it couldn't be edited directly.

When problems arose, proficient users almost became IT experts to figure out what particular part of the system was causing an issue, and pseudo-techno conversations were abundant:

- I've got Office 97, which version are you on?

- You saved it as an RTF, so where did the charts go?

- I'm on the XYZ domain, I can't see your file server.

Here Comes The Internet

In 2011, this is the stage that most companies are still at, despite the fact that computers are connected in a much more complicated way than LAN allows. As the Internet has developed and high-speed communication has crept into every workplace and most homes, this setup is creaking under the strain.

Internet access means users and their work are no longer confined to the desktop computer – now we have PDAs, Smart Phones, iPhones, Macs, laptops, set-top boxes, Internet kiosks – and this picture is getting more and more complicated.

The more common questions now are:

- How do I reach my PC from an airport kiosk?

- I need to place a client order from my iPhone.

- How can I be sure that this DOCX file doesn't have a virus?

Looking back, the one thing that's obvious is that we've been too focused on applications and hardware and not thinking about the actual work and the data. Why should it matter which version of Office you're using in the workplace when you want to update the company's budget on your home laptop?

So private and public networks have fused as we attempt to reach colleagues, employees and customers in physically separate locations. As this has grown, the weight on IT departments has become extraordinary. The networking complexity alone is staggering, considering the number of firewalls, VPN tunnels, switches and routers that allow all this to happen, and the number of security vulnerabilities grows with that complexity.

On the software side, there's also a wide range of clever products that enable remote computing, so users can sit at any Internet-connected device and 'see' the screen at home or work. Products such as Citrix, GoToMyPC.com or LogMeIn mask some of this complexity. But while remote software has been a major step forward, we are still at a hybrid stage where users have to consider the physical setup.

For the average user, she has a phone book of passwords, files all over the place, and the network – for all of its technological wonder – is stopping her getting work done. This hybrid is a hangover from the bad old days and is one of the major reasons that the next step in the evolution is happening.

The Security Problem

Right now, securing data is a task of labyrinthine proportions. Security used to be almost entirely physical: if you could secure a computer, a floppy disk, the print-outs and backup tapes, then data was secure. Just keeping people out of your office by placing a lock on the door provided the standard level of safety.

But the movement of data across networks has added many more dimensions. Now companies can lose their most sensitive information in a single email from an internal employee or a breach by a hacker. There are concerns about digital duplicates being left behind in the browser cache of public Internet kiosks or authorized users losing PDAs containing confidential information. Digital security is much more complicated than physical security, and many companies don't protect themselves to a high enough standard.

GOOGLE APPS SUCCESS STORIES

"Technically Google Apps can be up and running in a matter of minutes. Some universities offer services to just students and others offer to students, faculty, and staff." Among those universities that have embraced Google Apps is Abilene Christian University in Texas. The school dumped its own e-mail program in exchange for Google Apps in 2007, a move that has enabled the school to experiment with more advanced technology. The incoming fresh-man class this year will receive Apple iPhones or iPod Touches, a project that would not have been as easy had it not been for Google Apps, said Kevin Roberts, ACU's chief information officer.

http://www.pcmag.com/article2/0%2C2817%2C2326853%2C00.asp

An Introduction to Some of the Newer Trends

Google Apps is not a revolutionary step in software but rather builds on some of the trends that have emerged as the Internet has evolved.

Free Software

Google Apps is a free platform in its standard form, so it's worth talking about how free software emerged and rivaled applications that you previously paid for. Until recently, the concept of free software was hokey at best, and certainly not mainstream. Free software was the stuff of public domain groups and bulletin boards, written by enthusiasts and students, but could never challenge the work produced by professional teams of programmers in real tech companies.

It wasn't just that free software wasn't professional - even a decade ago, the idea that a free platform could be *better* than a paid solution was completely alien. People debate when this started to change, but I'd argue that the creation of the free operating system Linux and the 1998 release of Netscape Navigator's browser source code were pivotal moments.

Like a wave hitting a sand bank, the small ripple of these events magnified quickly and became a significant, visible force. It was the beginning of huge experiment in development collaboration, largely made possible by the Internet, where tens of thousands of programmers worked on parts of projects – for free in their spare time – to write software. They had effectively built programming teams, the virtual form of the paid groups at software companies, and it so happened that the software they produced was actually pretty good.

This evolved into the Open Source movement and became credible and respectable within a relatively short of space of time. In the next few years, corporate IT managers and hobbyists alike embraced the idea that 'free' and Open Source were not a threat or a back-door for substandard applications to enter organizations. Navigator improved over a decade to become the major competitor to Internet Explorer – Mozilla Firefox – which is currently the second most-popular browser in the world.

As free software has been embraced by users, major software companies have been forced to release free versions of their products just to ensure a position in the marketplace. Microsoft released Express versions of their Outlook email client, SQL Server database management system and Visual Studio development environment. Corporations still pay for the premium versions in order to receive support, but there's a clear change in the software pricing model.

Running in parallel with this trend is the fact that people want their data to work across different applications. It used to be that software locked and encoded data files so they only worked with that software but the rise of open standards has opened up the way your information is stored. Our view of data is changing: as users, we expect to access it anywhere, anytime, and with different applications. For example, I can send my Excel spreadsheet to a colleague using OpenOffice (a free version of Office) or Google Docs, and we can both access my work.

BUY NONE, GET ONE FREE

Is the business model of the future one where the customer no longer pays? Already products in the digital marketplace are being given away free, yet companies are still making profits."Digital economics changes our thinking about this. Everything that Google does is free to the consumer and yet Google is an extremely profitable company," says Chris Anderson author of 'Free: The Future of a Radical Price'. This new model still uses cross-subsidies - the idea that someone is paying - but in this case it's not you. "If you've grown up online, if you're of the Google generation, you intuitively understand that everything online is ultimately going to be free," says Mr. Anderson.

http://news.bbc.co.uk/2/hi/business/7811481.stm

The Rise and Rise of the Browser

Google Apps software runs entirely inside your browser with no installed software. When the browser first appeared, the notion that we could run full-blown applications in Netscape Navigator or the first versions of Internet Explorer was almost a leap into science-fiction. These tools really did little more than retrieve text files from a server somewhere and arrange the text and images on the screen with average levels of success.

The look and feel of web pages varied completely between different browsers and computers, and interaction was extremely primitive. Web pages lacked the immediacy or usability of regular applications since every user request took a round-trip to a server, and every resulting page was repainted on the screen - slowly. The web was useful for looking up news headlines or showtimes at a local movie theater but anything beyond that, especially in a business sense, wasn't really practical.

There have been a catalog of different technologies vying to change that experience but nothing really matched the desktop application environment. Also, web development was cumbersome in the browser's early years, and most companies were satisfied with a static web page that proved they existed, rather than trying to create interaction or dynamic content.

Users also had their fingers burned by browsers: people who previously had no clue what spyware or phishing even meant started discovering that people were trying to steal their passwords, identities and bank accounts. The media educated everyone to be cautious online and even the casual user today knows to look for the little padlock symbol before sending their credit card information into Cyberspace. So ultimately, the perception until recently was that the Internet was not a place for secure communications, stable software or business.

The rise of e-commerce has changed all this and the runaway growth of online sales is partly a result of a growing comfort level with sharing private data online (and partly by bargain hunting). The painful online shopping experience of yesteryear has been eclipsed by the slick user interfaces of modern retail sites like Amazon.com, and the juggernaut of commerce has brought every major retailer into a browser window.

Now we're in an environment where everyone talks about 'web 2.0', which officially ushers in the era of the browser. Facebook, LinkedIn, Yahoo! Mail, Twitter, Trip Advisor, Yelp, Open Table – more and more people now use rich applications within a browser. And these sites are fast, user-friendly, simple, and functional. Basically, if you can run JavaScript and store cookies (and by default you can), you're ready to roll on 99% of the most popular sites, with no pre-installed software or anything else. In fact, the browser is so agnostic about your computer system that any standards-based site will run quite happily on any device with an Internet connection, let alone just a Windows PC or an Apple Mac.

GOOGLE APPS SUCCESS STORIES

Businesses with less than 1000 staff should consider replacing in-house e-mail servers with webmail to reduce the cost of providing e-mail for end users, analyst firm Gartner has advised. Matthew Cain, research vice-president at Gartner, said companies with fewer than 1,000 seats would gain significantly from the webmail approach.

Geographically dispersed organizations and those that required less than 99% uptime should also consider the webmail model to simplify support and improve uptime, he said. Gartner has predicted that by 2012, webmail will serve the largest firms, with more than 50,000 seats. Construction firm Taylor Woodrow has begun using Google Apps to support collaboration for 1800 users.

http://www.computerweekly.com/Articles/2008/07/02/231325/gartner-says-webmail-cuts-costs-for-smes.htm

From network fog to "The Cloud"

You may have heard about 'Cloud Computing', and this is the next step. Google Apps is a cloud-based application – you access it from a browser and the actual software and data lives somewhere on the Internet that's always accessible (the cloud). Cloud computing is the natural evolution of the network, progressing from the Personal Computer (PC) to the Local Area Network (LAN), Wide Area Network (WAN) and finally the Internet. This is all caused by our need to share information and collaborate.

The concept of the cloud isn't simply the next iteration of networking – it's a total front-to-back revolution that's going to completely change the face of computing. The cloud is a metaphor for the complexity of the Internet, where dozens of computers chatter constantly so you can complete your call on Skype or send instant messages to friends around the world. But it's also so much more than that - it will fundamentally affect all our experiences with technology.

Think about some of the benefits:

- You're no longer tied to a single computer. You can access your applications or data absolutely anywhere.

- You can share whatever you like, whenever you like and work in real time with people anywhere on any device.

- It's not possible to leave your work documents at home or forget a flash drive containing some important spreadsheet, since the data follows you around.

This isn't science fiction, or an excitable sales pitch for software that doesn't exist. In fact, it's likely you are probably already using a cloud application or service. Critically, working in the cloud differs from the PC and network-centric world is two crucial ways:

- **It's user-centric**. As long as you remember your username and password, all your resources are immediately available. How many times have you been unable to finish work because your machine doesn't have the right software or you can't find a file that was emailed to you?

- **It's task-centric**. You can focus on what needs to be done rather than how to do it. Knowing you need Microsoft PowerPoint is not as important as knowing you need to finish your school presentation – the application is not as important as the data and the task.

Also, from a technical perspective, there are two radical shifts that result in major benefits for organizations: scale and remote access.

Scale: The Problem of Getting Too Big and Falling Over

Scale is simply a way of describing how technology functions (or doesn't) when you move from a single user to 1,000. Traditionally, this is challenging because you have to buy hardware and manage everything, and any major increase in demand has the potential to cause outages.

The problem is that a single user often requires as many server resources as 50 users, and then when user 51 is introduced, you need to double capacity to handle 100 users. There's a big step involved in moving from one band to another. When you have just a handful of users, as most small and medium-sized firms do, fundamentally it's like having to run a power station when you just want to use a toaster.

Cloud computing solves this invisibly – just as power stations do – by giving you the amount of attention you need at any point in time. The difficulty of making this work is taken away from you and your organization and handled centrally for everyone, which cuts your costs and ensures everything works when the number people using the applications increases.

Scale is still a problem for desktop applications such as email – for a 10-person company, a mail server and service contract are not cost-effective when split 10 ways. And at some point when you expand, you'll need another server and maybe a full-time IT person, which makes this service expensive. With Google Apps, whether you have 1 or 200 users, there is no equivalent problem since you don't need any servers, and you can implement everything in this book for a 2 or 20,000-person organization. How it really works behind the scenes is not really something to worry about.

GOOGLE APPS SUCCESS STORIES

The Daily Telegraph will migrate 1,400 seats over to Google's enterprise version of its business productivity software before the end of this year. Paul Cheesbrough, Telegraph Media Group CIO told IT PRO that "there was a five-to-one difference with Google in terms of the investment we would be making. And the Microsoft deal included only the software licenses and not the hardware or support that would have to come with it." He said that with so many journalists constantly on the move, Google Apps would allow staff to access email, documents and other information from anywhere. "The trial helped answer any questions we had about security, service levels and any risks associated essentially with running your business over the internet," added Cheesbrough. "It could be said that there's no better provider to do so than Google and we've found them hugely responsive."

http://www.itpro.co.uk/604644/telegraph-swaps-microsoft-office-for-google-apps

Remote Access: Getting to Your Data From Anywhere

The second radical shift is in remote access, which you get for free with browser-based applications. Remote access is a fancy way of saying that a computer not physically close to your software or data can still access those programs and files. As an example of where you normally see this, websites are the ultimate type of remote access:

- You can send photo albums to friends using services such as Picasa, Flickr or Photobucket.

- You can send invitations and manage events using Evite.

- You can blog on Wordpress or Blogspot from anywhere, and anyone in the world can see it.

In fact, we're so accustomed to using websites remotely that remote access is almost taken for granted. Yet to access applications from our company, school or university, we seem to accept that:

- You have to log-in through remote desktop to actually see your screen at work, or have to use some complicated secure VPN solution.

- You have to use a slow, third-party web-alternative that's completely different to the software you regularly use at your desk.

- Or, more often, you can't.

With Google Apps, your applications and data stretch beyond the boundaries of your office's front door and can be accessed in the exact same way from any device on the web just like a website. This is hard to imagine if you're used to desktop applications, but it's another revolutionary step we're about to take in the chapters ahead. Google Apps is like a rich desktop application that sets itself up whenever you open a browser, and it's completely independent of your physical location.

GOOGLE APPS SUCCESS STORIES

Looking just at the unplanned outages that catch IT staff by surprise, these results suggest Gmail is twice as reliable as a Novell GroupWise solution, and four times more reliable than a Microsoft Exchange-based solution that companies must maintain themselves. Gmail's reliability jumps to more than four times as reliable as a GroupWise solution and 10 times more reliable than an Exchange-based solution if you factor in the planned outages inherent in on-premises messaging platforms.

http://googleblog.blogspot.com/2008/10/what-we-learned-from-1-million.html

How Google Apps Solves These Problems

In exploring Google Apps, the value proposition is in taking all of this Office suite *stuff* out of your devices and networks and putting it somewhere else.

And it's not a major psychological leap - in the same way you don't know or care about where your Amazon.com shopping cart really exists, why should you be concerned about which version of Word you are using or where your company's Standard Legal Contract is stored? The promise of Google Apps is to simplify things and get back to focusing on what work you need to get done, rather than how you do it.

Now that we've talked about the promise of working in the cloud, it's time to roll up our sleeves and talk about Google Apps, it's strengths and weaknesses, and what it can do for you. We're now officially leaving the desktop behind, and getting into the Apps products and what they replace.

GOOGLE APPS SUCCESS STORIES

"We were looking for a technology that could be scaled immediately, and based on those metrics and the economic value of being able to roll out a technology super fast at a low cost, we decided to go with Google Apps."

Vivek Kundra – Chief Technology Officer, District of Columbia Government

Gmail: the flagship product

Prying into the world of Google Apps is probably easiest if we start with the email service, Gmail, since almost everyone uses email to some degree. Google introduced Gmail in March 2004, initially as an invitation-only service, and rolled out the product publicly in February 2007. The extraordinary buzz in the first couple of years caused a frenzied drive to find friends who could provide invitations.

For the first Gmail users, the experience was a radical departure from traditional email services and problems. Specifically:

- **Gmail isn't installed**: it's in your browser at http://www.gmail.com, and doesn't leave mailboxes on your machine.

- **Gmail is search-based**, so you retrieve messages using searches rather than folders. It offers sophisticated search methods, by overlaying the power and flexibility of Google's search platform, so you can find messages almost instantaneously among gigabytes and years of messages.

- **Gmail is conversation-based**, so threads of emails back-and-forth are displayed as a continuous dialog updated in real-time. Traditionally, each email appears as an independent item, making it difficult to link together threads of a conversation. Since many important emails are responses to other email, this makes conceptual sense and prevents out-of-sync responses.

- **Gmail is fast**, whereas prior web-based email services were mostly clunky and slow, Gmail acts like an installed application, offering interaction speeds that finally make web-based email viable.

- **The spam disappeared** and seeing that 80% of email is estimated to be spam, this is a major achievement. Among the variety of spam filtration systems, Gmail ranks as one of the best – their system learns from users identifying spam, and uses technology across their infrastructure to keep ahead of the spammers.

- **Gmail is free** and you can get started in minutes.

- **Gmail is continuously upgraded**: the platform keeps developing, with new features added by engineers regularly. When you log into Gmail, you automatically receive the very latest version, often without noticing. Contrast this with the desktop world - for companies like Microsoft, changing Outlook is complicated because of the way it's installed physically on millions of PCs. For Gmail, it's just another day at work.

Google Docs: the next step.

As email has emerged as a primary form of communication, it's also become a makeshift way to send documents – pictures, letters, spreadsheets, and PDFs – all conveniently attached and ready to read. Email attachments have become the main way to send files to groups of other people. Users send documents:

- Between work and personal email accounts so they can work outside the organizational network.

- To team members for review, comments or collaboration.

- To customers and vendors, to confirm pricing and legal contracts, or communicate marketing and new products.

This has worked as a simple way to share files but has severe shortcomings:

- When changes are made to documents, or you need to alert a group to imminent changes, this often results in mail storms where the current version of the information gets lost or becomes stranded across threads of a conversation.

- There's no way to revoke access to an attachment once its sent, so if you accidentally send a company's internal pricing list to the 'Customers' group, retraction is practically impossible. There's also no way of preventing or detecting how much this errant email gets forwarded around to unintended recipients.

- Real time collaboration is non-existent. Email has thrived as an queued form of communication, with messages waiting for you to read them, but there's no way for a group to make modifications to the same document at the same time.

There's nothing stopping you from using Gmail to send documents but Google makes it unnecessary with Docs, where you can create, edit and share documents online in a dedicated application, rather than using attachments. Docs simulates a subset of the functionality of desktop equivalents, and also enables users to import and export between desktop counterparts.

Docs doesn't mimic the interface of Microsoft Office to the same degree as OpenOffice and Zoho (Office users can transition to these with almost no training because their interfaces are so similar). There are major similarities but there are also simplifications meaning that most first-time Docs users find their feet within a few minutes of experimentation. We'll be walking through Docs in detail later on, but in the meantime you should think of Docs as being like a shared copy of Word or Excel in a browser.

Google Calendar: organizing your group.

Once you've solved communication with Gmail and collaboration with Docs, the next challenge is to organize and schedule people and events, which is the role of Google Calendar. Time-management software has been around for a long time, and has become much more sophisticated than a diary. Most desktop solutions enable you to:

- Add and modify meetings.

- Build recurring events.

- Print out schedules.

- Provide reminders – pop-ups and emails – for upcoming meetings, based upon a user-specified lead-time.

Google Calendar takes the functionality several steps further, and provides:

- Ownership and access to multiple calendars.

- Notification and syndication through SMS, RSS and embeddable widgets (don't worry if this doesn't mean anything yet).

- Discussion threads for events and integration with maps.

- Group-wide or world-wide publishing for calendars.

And, of course, there's the ability for you to access the calendar from anywhere and share calendars with people you chose, even if they are not part of your organization. The Premier version also offers resource scheduling, so team members can book meeting rooms or company cars without needing an assistant to manage a schedule. There's a tremendous amount you can do with the calendar application, but its core attraction is simplicity.

Google Sites: the easy way to build a website.

Sites is not designed to build a website in the traditional sense – it doesn't provide a public-facing view of your organization in a series of web pages. Yes, it could technically do this, but Sites is more concerned with producing a wiki or Intranet-style destination to foster collaboration, organization and productivity.

A wiki is simply a site that enables visitors to view and edit the content without a central editor managing these contributions. If you've used Wikipedia, the most famous wiki on the web, you can immediately see the effectiveness of the idea. Organizations have attempted to do the same thing with Intranet sites but these differ in several respects:

- A wiki can be built on-the-fly by users with no technical knowledge, and can be specific to a whole company, a department, a project or any collaborative effort.

- Once a user has the permission to access a wiki, their changes are published immediately without review.

- The layout and structure of a wiki is not fixed and can dynamically change according to the needs of its users.

Sites brings together all the Google Apps and you can integrate Docs, task lists, videos, presentations, files and other content. Sites can be arranged hierarchically and linked to each other, and the creator can decide their appearance and functionality. One Google Apps account can have multiple sites, and these can be shared with a select group or the entire world.

Sites is relatively new (released in February 2008), but it's a powerful part of Google Apps with almost limitless possibilities. Although it may sound daunting and complex, this App makes webpage construction simple, and we'll see later how you can build a site in less than five minutes.

Google Apps: the best of the rest.

When these individual applications first appeared, they often seemed designed to solve a niche problem, rather than forming part of an overall strategy. But when Google Apps was released, the underlying concepts became much clearer – the folks in Mountain View are trying to reboot our notions of how software works and bring all our different types of information together.

Other significant parts of the Google Apps suite include:

- **Google Chat**: a real-time messaging component that shows you the online status of your colleagues and friends, and enables you to send instant messages to each other.

- **Google Talk**: a voice-over-IP tool that allows you to make phone or video calls using a microphone or webcam, similar to Skype.

- **Message Security and Discovery (Postini)**: a highly-sophisticated message storage, policy enforcement and spam-blocking tool available in the Premier Edition. This is primarily focused on the corporate market but can be used by smaller businesses too.

Beyond these Google Apps components, there's also a host of other services available. Although this book doesn't cover these in any detail, here are some of the other tools that are available to you for free (with or without Google Apps) and can integrate with the overall suite:

- **Google Maps**: view maps, create directions, or build your own custom lists of items geographically (such as customer lists).

- **Google Earth**: explore the planet with this interactive program that includes satellite and 3D renderings of cities.

- **Google Product Search**: formerly known as Froogle, an aggregated view of the lowest prices for goods. If you're in retail, this is a great place to list your products.

- **Google Picasa**: store, manipulate and share photo albums, then access them from anywhere.

- **YouTube**: streaming video on the web – an easy way for your organization to host video media.

- **Google Pack**: a complete suite of essential desktop applications to help ensure standardized and commonly-used software is available on your machines.

- **Google Voice**: manage all your phone numbers in one location – this has just recently been added to Google Apps.

The most up-to-date list of the whole range of Google products appears at **http://www.google.com/intl/en/options**.

GOOGLE APPS SUCCESS STORIES

Genentech (a leading biotech company) turned on Google Calendar for its 12,000 employees last month. And even though Genentech expected a record number of helpdesk tickets to flood its "war room" given the size of the deployment, to the surprise of everyone, including Todd Pierce, the CIO of Genentech, the staff hardly heard a peep.

http://googleenterprise.blogspot.com/2008/11/innovation-its-in-genes.html

Thinking like a Googler: The power of search

People who work at Google are known as Googlers and it's helpful to adopt some of their concepts to get the most out of Google Apps. The good news is that these ideas make sense and help improve productivity; the bad news is that they can take a while to truly embrace. In addition to the idea of breaking down the barriers between different devices and overcoming network obstacles, there is one core essential theme: search. In the Google world, search is more powerful than organization. Here's why they might be right.

Whether working with files or email, we're accustomed to putting things in folders and places. This model of organization works well with one person, but starts to break down when several people are involved, since each person can have different organizational models. For example, one user might decide that this year's marketing budget spreadsheet should be in the Marketing folder, while another decides it belongs to Accounting, in a 'Current Year' sub-folder. The net result is that one of the users can't find a file because they use a different organizational model, and even if they can find it, the file might disappear when everything in 'Current Year' is moved to 'Last Year'. The same is true for email, since many people store messages by sender, by topic or project, and it's hard for collaborators to find data when they have competing organizational models.

This problem is solved when you take a search-based approached. Obviously, search has been central to the Google ideology from the beginning, probably because it may be the only way to catalog billions of web pages. In the website world, users are comfortable with the same approach. For example, if you are looking for restaurants in Manhattan, you wouldn't expect to drill down through an organized directory of Entertainment ▶ Eating Out ▶ USA ▶ New York ▶ Manhattan, since you've never been asked to do it that way before. You would most likely just type in 'New York restaurants' and expect the results to appear.

And so it goes for Google Apps:

- For Google Docs, you search on terms used within the document. Searching on 'marketing' or 'accounting' would both identify a marketing budget spreadsheet.

- For Gmail, while you can apply labels, a search will examine the text of every email in your entire history. A confirmation of a flight from San Francisco to Los Angeles would be found by searching for 'SFO' and 'LAX', rather than mining through travel and receipts folders.

One of the beneficial side-effects of the search approach is that users are no longer responsible for saving and deleting data. Google Docs is automatically saving all the time, and where it saves the information is not important to you as a user. There's also no pressure to clean-up anything since you have near-limitless space and the search algorithm automatically demotes older information. Instead of deleting emails to create space, you just need to archive them.

This is one of the biggest learning curves when you start using Google Apps, but once you become accustomed to search instead of organization, it makes much more sense.

GOOGLE APPS SUCCESS STORIES

Virgin America is the latest company to go Google and switch to Google Apps... all of the airline's 1,700 employees based across North America will be moving their corporate email to Gmail, and collaborating more efficiently using Google Calendar, Google Docs and Google Talk.

Their migration to Gmail will cut Virgin America's email system costs by about half on an annual basis, in addition to the long-term storage benefits where the move into the Google cloud will save them over 18 terabytes of space as the airline continue to grow and add employees.

http://googleblog.blogspot.com/2010/10/into-cloud-virgin-america-goes-google.html

How can Google Apps help my organization?

We've talked about some of the changes in the technical arena, and how Google Apps is one of the first application suites to harness the power of cloud computing. But in terms of the real concrete benefits, how can you really gain from using Google Apps?

Zero software and hardware cost

Typically, even providing just email requires the purchase of software licenses, exchange servers, spam filtering software and consulting services to configure. Adding a productivity suite such as Microsoft Office adds another major cost, since it is licensed per installation. As your organization grows, you are required to pay for new user licenses, upgrades, support and IT resources to solve problems along the way.

Google Apps involves no software installation whatsoever, and no additional server hardware or infrastructure. Remember that cloud services are independent of the users' computer, run in a browser and download themselves on-demand and invisibly to the user. This means the days of corrupted installations and missing software are over. Google Apps empowers you to distribute an entire productivity suite to up to 50 users without purchasing anything (or $50 per user per year for more than 50 users).

> If you choose to pay for the Premier edition, a flat fee of $50 per user per year covers the entire suite.

No upgrades ever needed

Software upgrades are a major headache for IT groups, especially in larger organizations — as users grow in number, the complexity grows exponentially. Types of operating system, hardware, custom user configurations and system availability are all barriers to providing users with the latest version, which is why most software vendors provide major upgrades infrequently.

Installations often have to be scripted for automated deployment, and building new machines is a time-consuming process. More often than not, software versions are not uniform within a single company, with some users and departments electing to remain on older versions and others insisting they remain on the cutting edge.

With Google Apps, upgrades are no longer a project in themselves since they happen constantly and automatically. All your users receive the latest versions with no interruption in service, and without IT staff having to work during weekends and other periods when users will not be impacted.

Increased reliability

'Uptime' refers to the percentage of time that a machine or service is usable. When an Exchange server or file server fails in your company, it has the capability of denying service to everyone since it can be the single point of failure. Google Apps boasts at uptime of 99.9% (which means the system may be unavailable for up to 9 hours a year).

Increased security

Data backups are usually made on a schedule - monthly, weekly or daily - but not instantaneously, so even with a good backup strategy it's possible to lose data between backups if a version of a file is deleted or unintentionally modified. Google Apps backs up the entire revision history of every document in real time in multiple locations – on-site backup will simply never be this good. Furthermore, there's no data physically stored at your site, so if computers are lost or stolen, or hard disks crash, your data is still safe (and inaccessible to third parties, in the case of hardware theft).

In terms of network security, communication with Google Apps happens over HTTPS, which uses SSL as an encryption mechanism so that traffic over public networks cannot be understood by unauthorized third parties. This is the same technology used by online banking and credit card processing.

Great support

Most desktop software support doesn't compare to the breadth and depth of support data at Google. There are forums, discussion boards, help centers – all maintained and updated constantly. For Premier and educational users, email and phone assistance is available 24/7, which is not common in the world of desktop software.

It's also worth mentioning that pushing applications into the cloud reduces complexity on your side, and helps reduce the need for support in the first place. The vast majority of helpdesk issues are related to a specific machine or software installation, and many of these disappear when there's nothing locally installed.

World-class collaboration

Collaboration has never really worked in traditional software because it involves emailing files or synchronizing groups of people, and it's hard to see what other users are working on. Google Apps takes a much simpler approach and enables users to see changes in real time. Literally, content changes before your eyes when another user is editing the same document. After five minutes of working on a spreadsheet with a colleague across the country, it's clear to see why this is so powerful and how multiple out-of-sync versions simply don't exist anymore.

What are the downsides of using Google Apps?

Of course, nothing exists without a downside. There are a number of problems with Google Apps that mean a cloud-based solution will not work for everyone. Some of these can be worked around while others may be show-stoppers.

- **No connection, no cloud**: you need an Internet connection to use Google Apps since it's hosted away from your network. When your Internet connection is down or you are working somewhere with no access, you have absolutely nothing. Although Google Docs has an offline mode and resynchronizes when you reconnect, basically you won't get very far without a connection. This is the biggest problem, but as Internet access becomes a ubiquitous utility, it's less of an issue. Still, if you live in area where you frequently lose connectivity, a desktop-based solution may still be your best bet.

- **Data Security**: although in many ways working in the cloud is more secure, there are some additional problems worth considering. There have been cases of hosted data going missing, but these are few and far between and vastly outnumbered by cases of data disappearing on a local file server. Still, you have to trust your data to Google, so there's inherently a risk in how Google protects that data.

- **User Security**: most breaches occur because users are lax about protecting their passwords and login sessions. Although there are high-profile stories about hackers intruding into private networks, the biggest risks are posed by users who have weak passwords. In a traditional network, these users are shielded by the physical security of your workplace. But since your network doesn't end at the front door when you use Google Apps, it's very important to educate users about logging out sessions, selecting strong passwords, and changing those passwords regularly (and not to share them). This is a serious issue – a third party that has obtained a user's password has access to all the real user's resources.

- **Social issues**: migrating users to a new platform is never easy and if your organization is married to Microsoft Office, it may be a Herculean effort to switch. Although I believe that the benefits in terms of productivity and cost savings justify investigating Google Apps, I'm realistic enough to know that not all organizations will embrace it.

Who should use Google Apps?

The functionality of Google Apps suits the vast majority of users' needs, and even groups who have never heard of the software should find it's easy to set up and use.

- **Individuals**: while our focus is on groups, let's not overlook the subset of users that we all belong to. Personally, I use the Google Apps suite in parallel with systems I use for work, including Gmail, Docs, Calendar and Sites. For a free, simple and powerful solution, there's nothing else that comes close.

- **Schools**: every student can benefit from Google Apps, which is quick to adapt and integrate into school projects. Write assignments in Docs, manage projects on Sites, get organized with Calendar and explore the power of gadgets – it's an ideal use-case.

- **Colleges and universities**: collaboration is really useful in these environments in a way that desktop applications cannot match. Since the educational edition is a free version of the Premier platform and offers powerful user provisioning features, it's rapidly being adopted by educational institutions worldwide.

- **Small businesses**: desktop licensing really cuts into the budget of small businesses and sole traders, and this group is another perfect target audience for Google Apps. As an added bonus, older PCs that struggle to run the latest versions of Windows and Microsoft Office can be reinstalled with Ubuntu Linux (a free operating system) and Firefox to run Google Apps. For more information, take a look at **http://www.ubuntu.com** for details.

- **Community groups**: another ideal target group, since they likely have no shared infrastructure and members uses their own PCs and personal email accounts. In this environment, Apps allows volunteers and members to collaborate seamlessly. There are many examples of soccer groups, minor leagues and community associations making excellent use of the Team Edition suite.

- **Large businesses**: Google itself uses Apps internally to run a multi-billion company, so I'm willing to bet that many other large corporations could do the same thing. Read some of the Success Stories inserts for examples of larger firms reaping the benefits.

- **Governmental bodies**: with the relatively new additional of state and federal security standards in the government edition, Google Apps is a great way to provide a rich featureset at a much lower cost per user to the taxpayer.

Who should not use Google Apps?

For the sake of full disclosure, there are some groups which Google Apps will not help. It's possible and even likely that this will change in the future, but for now the technology is not mature enough to warrant switching over. These include:

- **Offline or Internet-challenged users**: if you spend most of your day without a connection or you use dial-up, Google Apps will be a painful experience. A broadband connection is really a requirement, since the applications constantly use the network. While these users may tolerate the slowness of sending an occasional email, it won't take long for the frustration to be overwhelming.

- **Highly regulated organizations**: if your industry has strict regulations regarding network access and data security, it's possible that a Google Apps implementation will not comply. This is likely to change as cloud computing becomes the standard way to do business, but ultimately being in legal compliance takes precedence over productivity and cost-savings.

- **Users requiring security clearance**: as above, using Google Apps will most probably not be consistent with maintaining security clearance privileges. Due to Google security relying heavily on a username and password, this does not compete with biometric, PIN authentication technology and other safeguards commonly used. Google Apps has recently added OpenID and other mechanisms to make this more secure, so potentially this could change.

- **Office 'power users'**: Google Apps does not provide 100% of the Microsoft Office platform. If you're heavily dependent upon macros, advanced features, or tight integration with Access, Infopath, Groove or Outlook, then you are probably extracting the maximum value from your desktop licensing fees. Similarly, if you publish books for a living, Microsoft Word or Adobe InDesign will be a better solution than Google Docs. Having said this, you may find some value in some parts of Google Apps and may be able to adopt a portion of the platform, such as email or calendar.

- **Firms with a sunk IT cost**: in some cases, if you've paid for licenses of your existing office solution and don't have any ongoing maintenance or support costs, Google Apps *may* become an additional expense that's unnecessary. This is a corner case but nevertheless sometimes arises when firms compare the desktop and cloud environments.

I generally believe that each of these groups will eventually find a way into online software suites as they are developed, and cloud computing becomes more of a standard.

2. Getting started

Unlike traditional desktop software, Google Apps is platform independent, so it doesn't matter if you use a PC with Windows, an Apple Macintosh or Linux. In fact, anything capable of running a modern browser will be able to run Google Apps.

Before we start, you should ensure your preferred browser is updated to the latest version by visiting its respective download URL:

- Microsoft Internet Explorer (**http://www.microsoft.com**)

- Mozilla Firefox (**http://www.firefox.com**)

- Google Chrome (**http://www.google.com/chrome**), which incidentally I've found tends to provide the fastest performance for Google Apps software.

- Apple Safari (**http://www.apple.com/safari**)

- Opera (**http://www.opera.com/download**)

There are several steps involved in setting up a Google Apps account:

1. **Selecting the version** of Google Apps you want to use. There are subtle differences between each version.

2. **Signing up** for an account, either through your domain registrar's automatic setup, or using Google's manual account sign-up.

3. **Verifying ownership** of the domain in the case of manual setup. The services will not become active until this step is completed.

4. **Configuring DNS records** for your domain, which is usually fairly straightforward with most of the larger domain registrars.

5. **Administering Google Apps**, which includes setting up users, preferences and the Google Apps environment.

In this chapter, we'll look at each step in turn and the final administration step is covered in detail in Chapter 3. The process can take anything from minutes, in the case of a small company with no existing domain name, to days or weeks for a large organization with complex migration issues.

Selecting an edition

Originally, there were fewer variations between the different editions, but Google has provided additional features for specific user markets over time. The features can be broadly divided between standard and premier versions, with the premier versions offered in various flavors depending on the target market. Overall, there are currently six different editions of Google Apps:

- **Personal**: most commonly associated with the basic Gmail account. A personal account still provides access to most of the Google Apps software, though isn't strictly part of Google Apps. This provides a good starting point for new users wanting to experiment with the platform before committing any further. You can register for a free Gmail account at **http://mail.google.com**.

- **Standard business**: for companies with fewer than 50 employees and less complex infrastructures. This is a free, ad-sponsored version that restricts some of the more complex user-provisioning and security features. It's ideally suited to smaller businesses without IT departments or regulatory restrictions (such as email retention or enforcing minimum password requirements).

- **Premier business**: compulsory for companies with more than 50 users, and essential for those with more stringent security requirements. This version contains everything in the entire Google Apps platform. Google usually offers a 30 day free trial of this edition for new users.

- **Educational**: designed for Universities and K-12 schools, though otherwise identical to Premier. For schools and universities, the platform is free regardless of the number of users. Google's act of generosity here is a major donation to these groups, since their numbers can run into thousands of users, and the savings can be substantial. See **http://www.google.com/a/help/intl/en/edu/** for more information.

- **Non-profit**: again, the same as the Premier edition, but free for 501(c)3 non-profits with fewer than 3,000 users, and priced at 40% off for those with more.

- **Governmental**: a FISMA-certified version of Premier that secures data according to State and Federal standards, specifically designed for governmental organizations.

Additionally, here are some of the features to think about before deciding between standard and premier versions – but don't forget that you can switch versions at a later stage, so your selection is not final.

The Basics

The free versions are paid for by targeted ads in Gmail, but these appear as sidebars on your console rather than appendages in your email; you can disable these ads in any flavor of the Premier version.

In the personal version of Gmail, storage is limited to around 7.5GB (and grows continuously), whereas all Google Apps accounts have a fixed 25GB with the option of buying more space if needed. All versions have access to Gmail, Google Calendar, Google Docs and Google Sites.

Security and compliance

Increasingly, companies are required to store email messages for longer in order to respond to litigation and disputes. Traditionally this has been difficult and costly to do, and there have been many high-profile legal cases where important emails have gone missing. Gmail offers email security and archiving through Postini, a standard part of the Premier package, and provides a simple, reliable and automatic solution to the problem.

HTTPS is another feature to consider – all packages support secure traffic (SSL), but on the free personal or corporate version this is manually set in the dashboard configuration. Enforcement of SSL is standard in the premier versions, and it's even possible to prevent users from using non-SSL. This means that even if you frequently use public networks - such as wireless hot-spots in airports - the traffic is secure.

Premier also offers some additional controls over single sign-on (SSO), and the ability to set custom password strength requirements. Since user passwords are the primary security mechanism for accessing Google Apps services, this granular control over authentication will be essential for most corporate users. Additionally, Google Apps integrates with standard web single sign-on systems using the SAML 2.0 standard.

Support and integration

All versions have access to free self-service support but the Premier version provides email and phone-based help for critical issues. Only the Premier level provides a 99.9% uptime guarantee in the service level agreement, so in some respects the chances of actually needing support fall as you climb the feature curve.

There are a variety of advanced integration features that address the needs of most administrators – but these are all Premier features. With these, you gain access to Blackberry and Microsoft Outlook interoperability, tools to migrate your existing mailboxes and 'user provisioning', which is simply a way of controlling what users can access.

Signing up for services

Even if you are planning to sign up your company or organization for one of the paid Apps editions, it's a good idea to start with the basic free account to get a feel for the different applications.

With personal Gmail, there's no need for users to have their own domain name since the email addresses always appear as myusername@gmail.com. In the Google Apps versions, you are required to have a domain name, meaning that all email addresses become myusername@*yourdomain.com*.

The exact steps here depend on if you already own a domain name and, if you do, whether your domain registrar offers automatic setup for Google Apps.

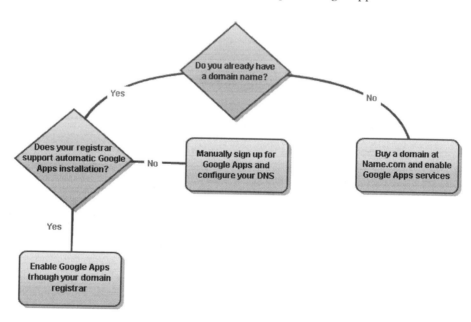

Automatic set-up with a domain name registrar

A domain name registrar is a company such as GoDaddy, 1&1 or Name.com, which is an ICANN-accredited entity enabling individuals and businesses to register domain names. Although this service is somewhat commoditized, many now offer additional services to help manage your domains, such as auto-renewal, private WHOIS and URL forwarding. Many of the most popular domain name companies also provide automatic configuration of Google Apps on their servers. While this process is limited to setting MX, CNAME and A records rather than creating individual user accounts, it can save some time and confusion especially for smaller organizations.

In the case of Name.com, you can either activate Google Apps at the time of registration, or from the Account Dashboard at a later point. If you already have a domain registered with Name.com, log in and visit their dashboard to view the list of your domains. From here, look for the "Enable" link in the Google Apps column (it will appear as 'Active' if Google Apps has already been configured):

Clicking this option will take you to the first step of a white-labeled sign-up page:

29

On this page, you should enter:

- **Contact information**: this is an email address outside of the domain, where Google can reach you for administrative messages (such as password resets).

- **Administrator account**: create your first administrative user in the new domain. This will be your initial user ID and password to gain access to the Google Apps dashboard. You can add additional administrative users later as required.

After completing this relatively simple form, you will have finished the initial set-up phase to establish Google Apps for the domain.

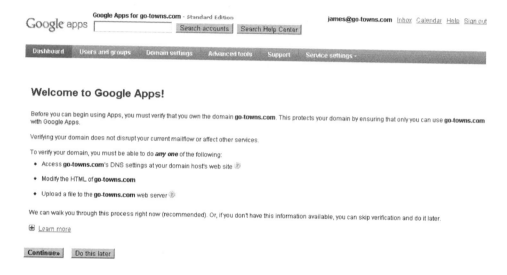

By using this automated setup, Name.com assigns the correct values to a range of CNAME, A and MX entries, which you can view from the DNS Management screen:

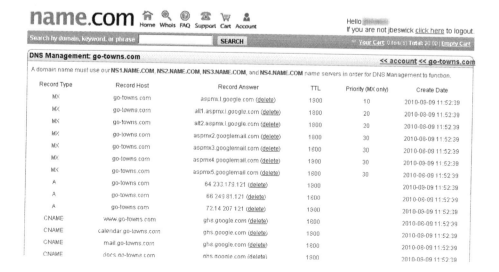

Signing up for Google Apps manually

Of course, if you don't already have a domain name or your registrar doesn't offer an automatic setup feature, it's also simple to activate Google Apps manually. To get started, the official website is located at **http://www.google.com/a/**:

- **For a Standard (free) account**: hover over the Apps Editions menu and click 'Standard'. From here, click 'Get Started' to begin the sign-up process.

- **For a Premier (paid) account**: click 'See details and pricing' and then select 'Begin Free Trial' on the next page.

The following screens show the sign-up process for the Standard edition - the Premier version varies slightly and requires payment information. There are two options from here:

31

- **Use an existing domain name**: if you're already the owner of a domain (e.g. mycompany.com), select this to use this domain for Google Apps services. Choosing this option does not have any effect on your current email or website(s) if they are already in place - at least, not at this point.

- **Buy a domain name**: if you either don't have a domain name or you want to buy a test domain to try Google Apps before committing, click this option.

In the first case, enter the domain and click 'Get Started' - we'll catch up with the purchase option shortly.

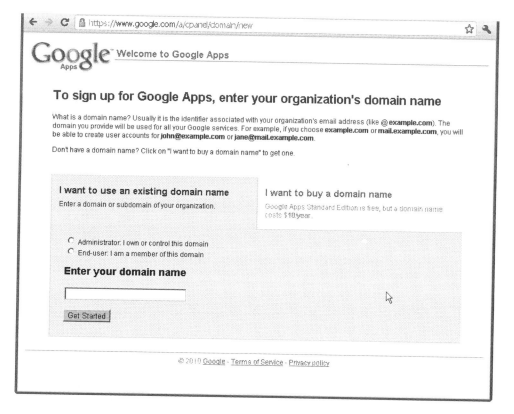

The sign-up form for an existing domain is fairly straightforward - you are providing contact details as the account administrator and some general information about your organization. Make sure these details are accurate, since if you forget a password or have any other problem, what you provide here will be used to verify your identity.

Once you have completed the form, click **Continue** to advance to the final set-up screen.

Google™ Welcome to Google Apps

1. Choose a domain name	**2. Sign up**	3. Set up

Sign up for Google Apps Standard Edition (step 2 of 3)

Google Apps Standard Edition is limited to **50 user accounts**. Interested in more user accounts or other advanced features? Try Google Apps Premier Edition for free.

Information for ekcy.com

* indicates a required field

Account Administrator

First name *	James	(e.g., Jane or John)
Last name *	Beswick	(e.g., Doe or Smith)
Email address *	james@oneuproar.com	Please enter a **valid** email address.
Phone *	415-555-5555	(e.g., 123-456-7890)
Country/Region *	United States	
Job title	Author	(e.g., President or Systems Administrator)

Google Apps requires changes to DNS to properly set up services. Learn more

☑ * I understand that if I cannot alter DNS records for my domain, I may impact my organization's ability to use Google Apps

Organization Information

Organization name Ekcy (e.g., ProkomCo or Tyrell Corporation)

Type Business

Size of organization 1 - 5

Does your organization currently provide email accounts?
○ Yes
◉ No

If so, what does your organization use for email?

_____ (e.g., Microsoft Exchange)

Has our sales team assisted in your decision to sign up for Google Apps?
○ Yes
◉ No

[Continue]

Now create your first administrative user in the new domain. This will be your initial user ID and password to gain access to the Google Apps dashboard. You can add additional administrative users later as required.

After completing the CAPTCHA test and accepting the Terms and Condition, click **I accept** to finalize the creation of the Google Apps account for this domain. You will soon receive a welcome email with details about the next steps of activation, together with the URL to access your Google Apps dashboard, which is in the format **http://www. google.com/a/yourdomain.com**.

Verifying domain ownership

If you didn't purchase the domain through Google or use the automatic setup provided by your domain registrar, you will need to verify that you are the domain owner.

This step does not apply if you use the automatic setup at your registrar or if you purchased the domain through Google Apps.

When you first log into your Google Apps dashboard from the link provided in the welcome email, you'll see the following page:

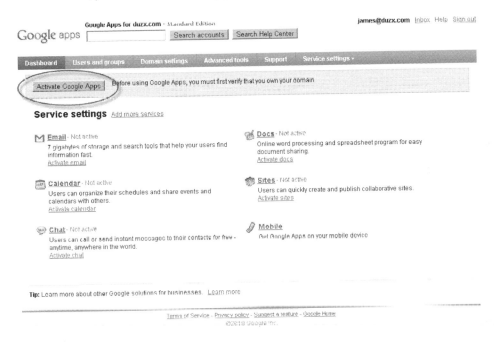

Click on **Activate Google Apps** to begin the activation process, which uses one of two mechanisms to prove you have administrative access to the domain name:

- **Upload an HTML file** to your domain: if you have web-hosting for your domain and have FTP access, this is the easiest method. However, this is not possible if you don't have any web space for files.

- **Add a CNAME entry**: Google Apps will provide a CNAME value on the next page - take a note of this, as you will need to give this value to your registrar.

The exact steps for adding a CNAME vary by domain registrar, and Google provides instructions for the most popular here: **http://www.google.com/support/a/bin/answer. py?answer=47283&topic=9196**.

Creating the CNAME can take 24-48 hours to propagate through the Internet's DNS servers, so press the 'Verify' button on the Google dashboard and wait for confirmation. By creating this sub-domain, you have proven to Google that you own the domain. When verification is complete, the full range of services will become active in the Dashboard.

> **At this point in the manual setup, you have signed up for Google Apps on your selected domain and proven ownership. Email is not yet configured.**

Configuring DNS records for your domain

A domain name is simply a pointer for Internet traffic, and behind each domain name exists a routing table that provides further information. The DNS records only have to be set if you didn't use automatic setup with your registrar, or you didn't purchase a domain name through Google.

There are various types of DNS record that affect Google Apps:

- **A** records: these indicate the underlying IP address for web server requests.

- **CNAME** records: most commonly associated with sub-domains, which we will use to set access to Google Apps services (e.g. **http://mail.yourdomain.com**).

- **MX** records: determine how mail traffic is handled and where it goes. Without MX configuration, any email sent to mydomain.com will go nowhere.

> **If you already have active email services, this part of the process may cause disruption during the switch-over.**
>
> **If you do not have the authority to change your organization's email and web server records, <u>STOP HERE</u> and consult your IT department!**

If you read the previous warning and have decided to change your MX records anyway, thus moving your email services away from your current provider, then this section will get Gmail working for your domain.

When email is sent to your domain, the domain name system provides a mail exchange (MX) record which specifies the onward route of the email. Consequently, if you change your email host, your domain name stays the same but behind the scenes a new list of servers is handling the mail.

Go your Google Apps Dashboard and click the **Activate email** link to continue:

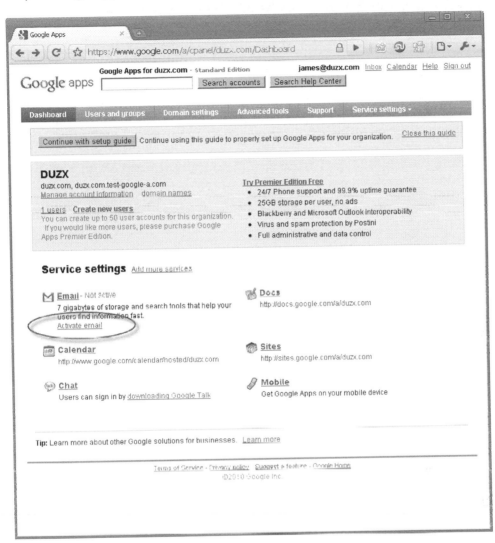

Use the drop-down to select your hosting company's specific instructions - if your company is not listed, you should contact their technical support if you are not familiar with modifying MX records, since an error at this stage can prevent any existing email configuration from working.

Add each of the MX server addresses and priority values in turn, then come back to this screen and click **I have completed these steps** when you are ready.

Set up email delivery

Changing Mail Exchange (MX) records

Mail Exchange (MX) records control how incoming email is routed for your domain. Before Google can host your email, you'll need to change these MX records to point to our servers.

⚠ **If your domain already has email addresses,** please be careful changing MX records. To avoid disruption in email service, be sure to create the same set of user accounts with the control panel before changing your MX records Learn more

If you're not ready to change your MX records yet, use the temporary email address (<username>@duzx.com.test-google-a.com) assigned to your user accounts when you create them. The temporary email address will be deactivated once you change the MX records. You must also verify domain ownership before using any Google Apps.

Showing instructions for [Any hosting company ▼]

1. **Sign in to your domain hosting company's website** using the username and password associated with your domain.

2. **Navigate to an MX record maintenance page.** MX records are special DNS (Domain Name Service) records, and are often located under sections titled "DNS Management," "Mail Server Configuration," or "Name Server Management." You may need to turn on advanced settings to allow editing of these MX records.

3. **Delete any existing MX records** before entering new MX records.

4. **For each MX record, enter information according to the entries in the following table.**

   You may not be allowed to enter the priority values exactly as they appear in the table below; in that case, simply ensure that the server addresses are prioritized in the same order as they appear in the table. (i.e. The priority ranking [1, 3, 3, 5, 5, 5, 5] should work just as well as [1, 5, 5, 10, 10, 10, 10] so long as you keep the addresses in the right order.)

   If you're asked to specify the type of each record you're adding, enter "MX".

   MX records often require the specific format of DNS records, including a trailing dot (".") at the end of any full-qualified domain names (e.g. "server.example.com.")

   Set any TTL values to the maximum allowed.

MX Server address	Priority
ASPMX.L.GOOGLE.COM.	10
ALT1.ASPMX.L.GOOGLE.COM.	20
ALT2.ASPMX.L.GOOGLE.COM.	20
ASPMX2.GOOGLEMAIL.COM.	30
ASPMX3.GOOGLEMAIL.COM.	30
ASPMX4.GOOGLEMAIL.COM.	30
ASPMX5.GOOGLEMAIL.COM.	30

5. **Change the SPF record to fight SPAM** (optional)

   You may define the SPF record to authorize only certain IP addresses to send email for your domain. This will prevent spammers from sending unauthorized email under a forged address from your domain.

When finished, click on "I have completed these steps" to have Google check your MX records.

[I have completed these steps]   [I will do this later]

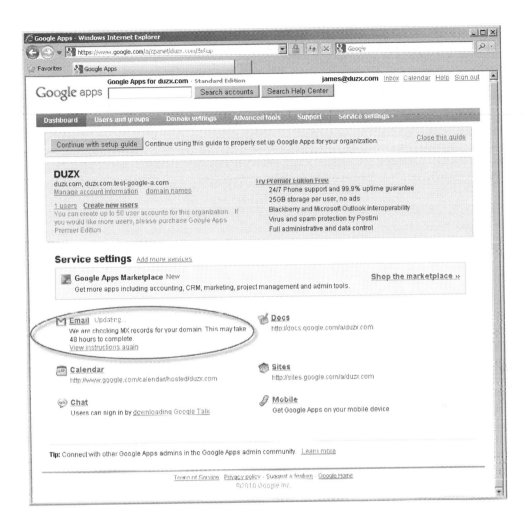

After completing the MX entry, the dashboard screen indicates that Google is checking the new configuration. Although this can take up to 48 hours complete, it typically happens much more quickly.

At this stage you have successfully signed up for Google Apps with your domain, created one administrative user, and started the process to route email through the Apps platform. In the next chapter, we will configure your new Google Apps domain and look at adding additional users, migrating their existing data, and setting up some of the advanced services.

> For a basic guide to DNS terminology, visit http://www.google.com/support/a/bin/answer.py?hl=en&answer=48090.

Selecting a password

Your password is the key to all Google services and data in your account, and having this password compromised opens all your data to a third party. This is bad enough for personal email, but for business or organizational use, it could be catastrophic. Contrary to popular belief, most passwords are cracked by guessing rather than any high-tech trickery, so make life a little harder for anyone trying to access your account by following these rules:

- **Don't be obvious**: while it sounds obvious in itself, picking the name of a family member or pet, or your favorite football team is almost as bad as just selecting 'Password'.

- **Don't use an existing online password**: while you may have passwords to many sites, don't duplicate across them. If someone learns your password to Linked In or YouTube, it will at least stop them from accessing all your online accounts.

- **Don't use a regular word**: dictionary attacks are a standard way to break into accounts, which involves using a computerized dictionary to try every word. Even long words like 'difficulty' are not hard to break.

- **Mix cases, numbers and punctuation**: your password becomes almost impossible to guess if you combine from all the character sets on the keyboard.

- **Change your password regularly**: using the same password for years only increases the chance that it's discovered, while changing it every day becomes laborious. Choose a sensible time period that balances security with ease-of-use.

- **Don't share your password or write it down**: treat it like your ATM pin.

One approach, since most people have trouble remembering meaningless strings of characters, is to take a regular word and interchange letters with numbers and punctuation. For example, taking the word Georgia (not secure), you could transpose letters to create <ge0Rg1A> (very secure).

Finally, having said all of this, don't forget that emails sent to others are not necessarily secure, because you don't know what happens to the message one it leaves Google (and of course the other person may have a weak password). Never send social security numbers, credit card numbers or highly sensitive information through email. This applies on other email systems and not just Gmail.

Frequently Asked Questions

Do I need a domain name?

Not for a personal Google account, which provides access to Gmail and Google Docs, but a domain is required to use Google Apps as a multi-user suite for your organization.

How do I get a domain name?

You can purchase a domain name through any domain registrar, which acts as an intermediary between ICANN (a non-profit corporation that manages the assignment of domain names) and the end-user. Popular registrars include GoDaddy, 1&1 and Name. com, although there are many others. Registering a domain costs around $10 a year and takes 24-48 hours to become fully active across the Internet. You can also purchase a domain during the sign-up process with Google Apps.

Can I use an existing domain name?

Yes, by telling Google which domain you would like to use in the sign-up process, verifying your ownership of that domain, and then making the appropriate changes to the CNAME and DNS records as discussed in this chapter.

Do I have to use my company's primary domain?

No, there's nothing to stop you registering a new domain for the sole purpose of Google Apps and leaving your existing website resources untouched. The major downside is that your email addresses will represent your second domain rather than the primary, although in the next chapter I'll show you how to have more than one domain per email address to circumvent this problem.

Can I change which edition of Google Apps I use?

Yes, you can upgrade from Standard to Premier at any time by paying the $50 per user per year license fee (usually, Google Apps Premier also features a free 30-day trial, after which you can choose to upgrade or remain on the free edition). You can also downgrade from Premier to Standard.

How do I access the Google Apps administrative dashboard?

Open a browser and enter the URL **http://www.google.com/a/yourdomain.com**, replacing *yourdomain.com* with your actual domain name.

Can I split my users between two different versions of Google Apps?

No, there currently no way to host two versions on the same domain name, though you can have two versions on separate domains.

If my data is stored with other users' data on the same server, how is it secured?

Google has controls in place to virtually separate customer data, so you can't see other people's information and they can't see yours. These controls, which are similar to those used by banks to protect customer accounts, have passed a SAS 70 Type II audit.

Where is my data physically stored?

The benefit of using the cloud is that you don't really need to be concerned where the software or data is really residing. But in reality, Google has a network of data centers that balance the load and performing back-ups of your information in multiple locations. The addresses of these data centers is kept private for security reasons.

Can I keep my existing website and use Google Apps?

Yes, although this can only be completed manually by ensuring that your domain's 'A' record is not changed when you activate Google Apps. You can still add CNAME records to set up sub-domain access, so for example http://mail.yourdomain.com would route to Google Mail. However, you should make sure that the A record for both *.yourdomain.com and yourdomain.com are set to the IP address where the site is hosted.

Can I force my users to use strong passwords?

In the Premier Edition, you can set password policies to help prevent users from selecting weak passwords. This feature is not available in the Standard Edition.

3. Administering Google Apps

Once the previous four steps in chapter 2 have been successfully completed, Google Apps will become operational with all its default settings and one user (the administrative user you defined during the sign-up process).

In this chapter, we'll look at the final steps needed to configure the Google Apps platform, including:

- **Creating users**: there are several different ways to add new accounts to your Google Apps domain.

- **Managing user groups**: configuring system-wide user groups and setting appropriate roles and permissions.

- **Domain settings**: a tour of the domain-wide settings available, which should be implemented before rolling out the platform to your users.

- **Service settings**: modifying options for each underlying application, together with setting maximum visibility options and general defaults.

To get started, open a browser and navigate to **https://www.google.com/a/yourdomain.com** (replacing yourdomain.com with your actual domain name):

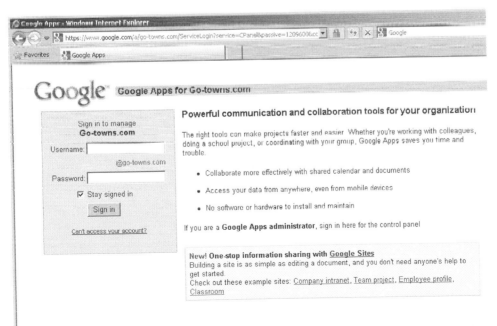

After entering the user ID and password you used in chapter 2, you will see the Google Apps administrative dashboard:

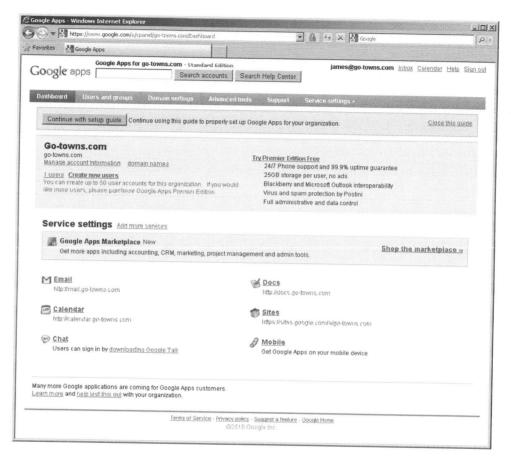

This provides a summary of your Google Apps services at a glance and shows:

- **Navigation** to all the major features of the dashboard.

- **Administrative messages**. When you first start, this will show links to help resources such as the setup guide, but will also provide details of outages, news announcements, and anything else that's important for administrators.

- **The top banner**, which shows the number of users in your plan, the domains that are linked, and promotions for the Premier Edition if you're using Standard.

- **Services**: shortcuts to all the services available in your chosen edition, along with access URLs, which will either be the sub-domains you created in chapter 2 or the generic access URLs.

Let's step through each of the menu items in turn to configure Google Apps.

Creating Users

Creating users one at a time

Initially, you are the only user in your Google Apps domain. If you only have a small number of users in your organization, it's often easier to create their accounts one at a time. Click on the *Organization & Users* tab in the Control Panel to access your user list.

Click **Create a new user** to start creating accounts. In the resulting dialog, all three fields are compulsory and you can optionally have Google create temporary passwords for users or define a password by clicking **Set password**.

> By default, Google will assign a temporary password - this is the more secure method, simply because it's better practice to restrict the knowledge of user passwords to a single person.

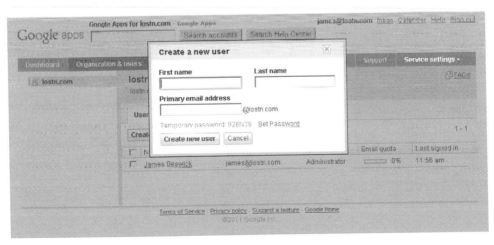

Click the **Create new user** button to finalize the account creation. The next page allows you to print set-up instructions for users or have them emailed to an alternative email address.

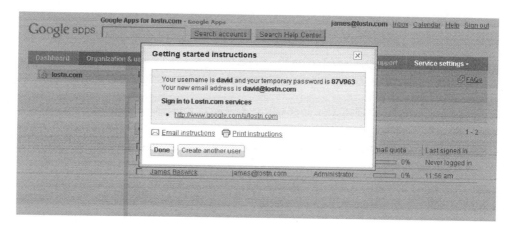

These steps produce a basic, non-administrative account with fewer permissions than the top-level account you used to sign up for Google Apps. Later on, we'll see how you can promote other users to have administrative rights, and you can monitor or suspend user accounts as needed.

Click **Create another user** to create more accounts, and once finished, you should see the entire list when clicking **Back to user list**. Don't worry if you haven't set up everyone, since you can add additional accounts from the dashboard at any time.

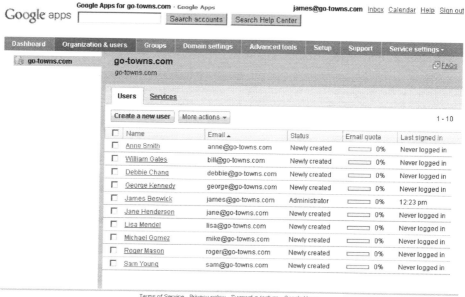

Creating multiple accounts simultaneously

If you need to create a large number of user accounts, click **More actions ▶ Bulk upload users** from the **Organization & Users** screen to avoid having to set up each one manually.

The method requires a CSV file, which you can create in Excel or Notepad (or any other spreadsheet program or text editor), formatted to the specifications above. In Excel, simply enter the required in headings in row 1, followed by each user account:

	A	B	C	D
1	email address	first name	last name	password
2	anne@go-towns.com	Anne	Smith	878976
3	george@go-towns.com	George	Kennedy	435435
4	sam@go-towns.com	Sam	Young	784674
5	lisa@go-towns.com	Lisa	Mendel	543556
6	bill@go-towns.com	William	Gates	567547
7				

You must enter a password in column D, although you can force users to change the password upon their first login by checking **Require a password change**.

Once the CSV file is ready, click **Browse** to locate it and then click **Upload and Continue** to process. Depending upon how many accounts are in your file, this can take anything from a few seconds to several hours (for thousands of users), and you will receive an email once the accounts are ready.

To create random passwords in your Excel file, use the formula **=RANDBETWEEN(100000,999999)** in the cells in column D to create a six-digit code for each account. This is preferable to setting the password to a static value (like 'password') because it prevents users from guessing passwords for accounts that haven't logged in yet.

For very large numbers of users, there's the Google App Provisioning API which you can use to integrate your Google Apps with your existing identity systems, like Microsoft Active Directory. This requires programming or assistance from a Google Apps Solutions Provider, and is the recommended user setup method for large corporations or schools.

Managing an individual user's account

Administering user accounts often involves, unsurprisingly, quite a few administrative tasks such as resetting passwords and suspending accounts. Fortunately, this is easy in Google Apps. To make changes to any account, select the user from the user list page:

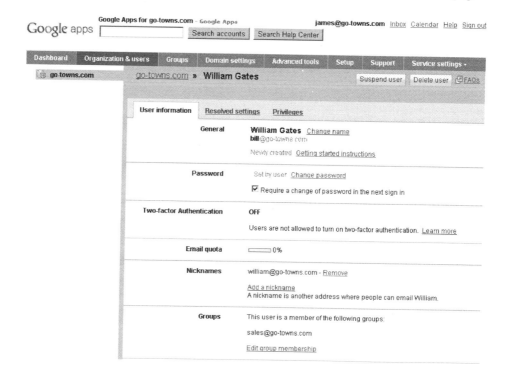

From this screen, you can:

- **Change their name**: which will propagate through all Google Apps services.

- **Suspend the account**: this prevents the user from logging in or receiving new email or notifications, but leaves all their data intact. You would typically suspend an account if an employee believes their password has been compromised, or other suspicious activity happens.

- **Delete the account**: this will remove all their messages and data within 5 days. If the user owns spreadsheets or other assets, these will also be removed unless you reassign ownership (see Chapter 6 on Google Docs).

- **Change the password**: users can change their own passwords while logged in, but if they forget their password then an administrator can set a new one here.

- **Create a new administrator**: checking the 'Privileges' box will make a user an administrator with all the same access rights as your account.

- **Add a nickname**: this is another address for the same user, for example william@go-towns.com instead of bill@go-towns.com. Both addresses will work identically for the purposes of receiving email. Since the original user ID cannot be changed, this is the easiest way to correct an error to an existing user without deleting and recreating an account.

Managing User Groups

Groups provide a convenient way to send messages to several people at once, separated by department, function, project or any other grouping. For example:

- **Accounting group**: could contain everyone in the accounting department.

- **Managers group**: may consist of all employees who manage staff.

- **Apps-Rollout group**: encompasses everyone involved with rolling out Google Apps to your company (a project-focused team).

- **Sales group**: may represent all personnel who should receive incoming sales-related emails.

- **Everyone group**: consists of every employee (i.e. all Google Apps users in your domain).

While you are probably familiar with groups if you have used Microsoft Outlook or Lotus Notes before, in Google Apps they extend beyond email communication to:

- Inviting groups to meetings

- Sharing calendars

- Sharing documents, sites and videos

A group can be created, maintained and deleted by an administrator, and there are some differences between the Standard and Premium versions:

- **Creator**: in the Standard edition, all groups must be created by an administrator, whereas the Premium versions allow users to create groups by themselves.

- **Size**: standard allows up to 100 members of each group - Premium is unlimited.

- **Number**: you can only create up to 10 groups in Standard - again, Premium is unlimited.

Creating a new group

To create a new group, click **Users and Groups** from the dashboard and select the **Groups** tab. The first time you use this feature, there are no existing groups shown, though normally you would see all the domain's groups on this page.

From here, click **Create a new group**:

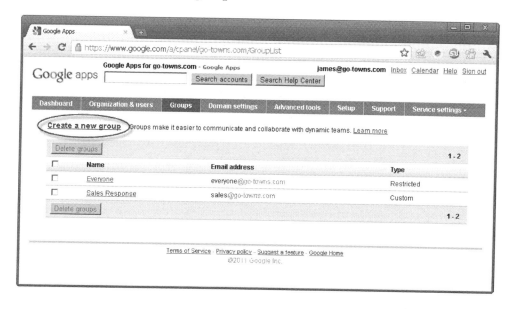

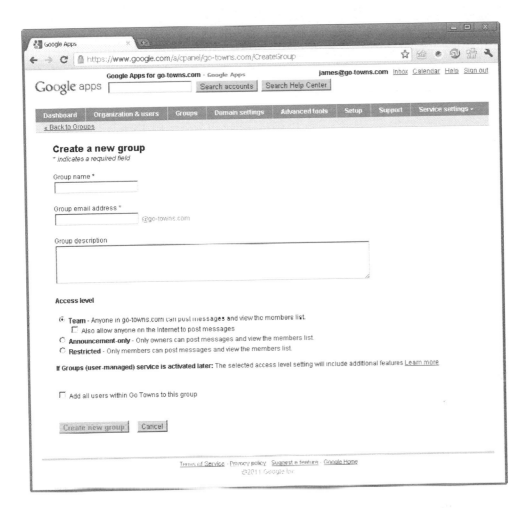

The first two fields are compulsory and self-explanatory - the optional third helps explain the purpose of the group. The access level is worth covering in more detail:

- **Team**: all group members can send messages to the group and see who is in the group. If the checkbox is selected, then any group members outside the domain can also post messages. Most groups use this setting.

- **Announcement only**: members can only receive messages and cannot see other members. This is most useful for company announcements and news.

- **Restricted**: in this model, the group is not accessible to anyone outside the group. Non-group members cannot send messages to the group or see its members. This is best for teams that do not operate with anyone outside their group.

The access level can be changed at any time - in most cases, it's easiest to start with 'Team' level access and then become more restrictive as necessary. Click **Create new group** when you are ready.

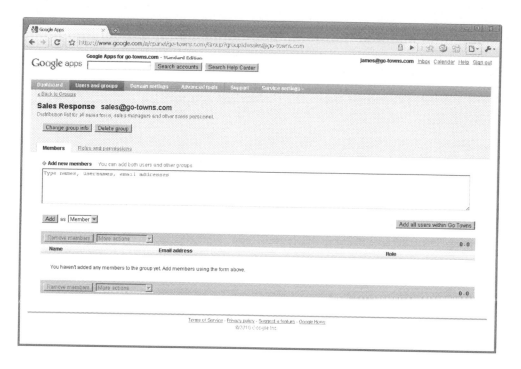

In the next step, we can define the members of the group, and there are several important points to note here:

- **External users**: a group can also include people outside your domain. For example, you could create a group for each client project (client1@mydomain. com), and actually include your clients' email addresses as part of the grouping. Consequently, any messages sent to client1@mydomain.com would reach both internal and external users.

- **A group can contain another group**: a college with freshmen students may have a group called *freshmen*. This group may then be added to an *undergraduates* group. Any new members added to *freshmen* would automatically become part of the *undergraduates* group; conversely, any that leave would automatically be removed.

- **A user can either be a member or an owner**: a member can participate in the group in the manner defined by his or her access level. An owner has the ability to modify membership and group attributes, effectively acting as an administrator for the group.

You can also choose to have all domain users added to the group by clicking the command button above the membership list. Once the group is created, anytime you use its name in other parts of Google Apps, all members of the group are included automatically (as we'll see in subsequent chapters on those services).

Deleting a group

Navigate to the **Groups** tab to display a list of existing groups. To delete a group, place a checkbox next to its name and click **Delete groups**:

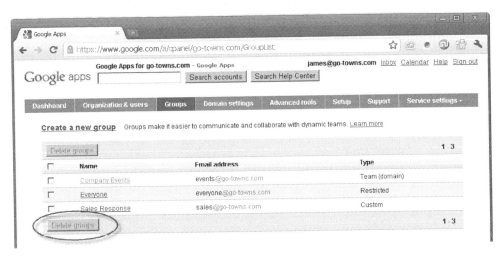

Deletion is permanent, though it does not delete the underlying user accounts or any messages, documents or assets that were associated with the group. If the group was configured as a mailbox, a feature only available in the Premium editions, any messages sent to the group will bounce back to the sender after deletion.

Sharing contacts between users

To turn on this feature, navigate to the **Domain Settings** tab, and then the **User settings** tab to see the contact sharing default. When contact sharing is enabled, this is the same as using a global address book, so users in the domain have access to each other's contacts. This can be disabled by selecting the lower option and clicking **Save changes**.

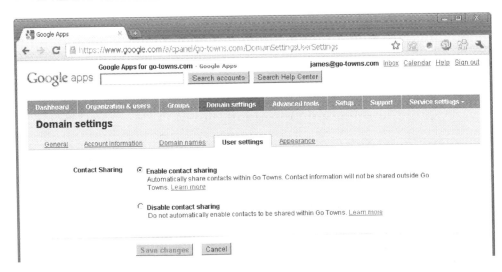

Domain Settings

The domain settings tab provides access to a range of site-wide features that affect all your domain's users.

General tab (see next page):

The main settings break down into the following groups:

- **Contact information**: each domain can only have one primary administrator, who is defined here. You should provide a secondary email address hosted outside of the Google Apps domain so that you can reset the password if it is ever lost or forgotten. Without this, you will need to contact Google Apps technical support if you are ever locked out.

- **User support message**: provide a generic support response here in order to streamline the handling of support cases. If your organization has a small number of users, this will typically contain the contact information for your IT resource. If you have a dedicated team or external support center, you might provide more detailed information about how to raise tickets, and the expected response time.

- **Time zone**: select your country of residence, and if your users are all in one time zone, select the appropriate entry. If your users are scattered geographically, leave this blank so each user can set a preference.

- **SSL**: for most organizations, it's wise to enable this option, though it causes a very slight drop in performance. If your users frequently use wireless connections or public connections, HTTPS prevents eavesdropping or unauthorized account hijacking. Personally, I would strongly suggest always enforcing SSL, regardless of your organizational size or networking setup.

- **New services and features**: Google frequently releases new services as part of the Apps suite. If you want to gain access to these automatically, check the box to add new services as they become available.

- **Pre-release features**: Google is also famous for their beta-release features, which provide customizations and extra options - but without support or guarantees. Enable this option to beta test Google's latest ideas, but be prepared for potential instability and rough edges.

- **Advertising**: this can be disabled in the Premier edition, but not in the Standard versions. Most organizations using Premier choose to turn off advertisements.

Google apps   [   ] [Search accounts] [Search Help Center]

| Dashboard | Organization & users | Groups | Domain settings | Advanced tools | Setup | Support | Service settings ▾ |

Domain settings

General   Account information   Domain names   User settings   Appearance

Organization name   [Go Towns]

Contact information   Designate contact email addresses for service communications, including payment notifications, and any opt-in subscriptions.

Primary administrator account
[james] @go-towns.com

Secondary email address
[james@415systems.com] (email address must be outside this domain)

☑ In case of forgotten administrator password, send password reset instructions to secondary contact.

User support   Provide a note to your users in case they need help (like a password reset instruction).
Note: This note will be publicly accessible. Learn more

[text area]

Language   Default language for users at Go Towns:

[English (US)   ▼]

Time zone   Default time zone for users at Go Towns:

[Show all timezones   ▼]
[(GMT-08:00) Pacific Time   ▼]

SSL   ☑ Enable SSL
Automatically enforce Secure Socket Layer (SSL) connections when your users access Gmail, Calendar, Docs, and Sites. Learn more

New Services and Pre-release Features   ☑ **Automatically add new services when they become available**
If you select this option, you won't need to manually add new services for users to access them.
Learn more

☑ **Enable pre-release features**
If you select this option, your users automatically receive new Google features in a pre-release state as soon as they are available to consumers. Otherwise, your users receive new Google features shortly after the consumer launch, on a predictable release schedule. Learn more

Control panel

○ **Current version**
Current control panel features are available in many language settings. Learn more

⦿ **Next generation** (US English only)
New control panel features will be available to you a little earlier than with the current version.
Learn more

News, feedback and promotions   ☐ Receive occasional email notifications about new services or features.

☐ I am willing to be contacted about this product and my experiences.

Unsubscribe from all marketing and non-transactional emails
You will be unsubscribed from non-transactional emails regarding enterprise products from Google.
Unsubscribing will override the email notification and feedback options above.

[Save changes] [Cancel]

Account information tab

Here you can switch between the Standard and Premier editions, purchase new user accounts, control billing, and generate a support PIN if you need to call Google for support issues (Premier edition only). You can also cancel your account if you so choose.

Domain names tab

Many organizations have multiple domains that all point to the same content – for example **http://www.google.com** and **http://www.goog.com** will both lead to the same familiar homepage. If your customers frequently confuse or intermingle two or more domain names, this feature ensures that mail continues to reach users configured for the primary domain.

For james@mycorp.com, if I add mycorporation.com as a domain alias then all mail sent to james@mycorporation.com will still reach the mycorp.com mailbox. For each domain you add, you will need to verify domain ownership first (see Chapter 2).

For Premier edition users with Postini activated, adding domain aliases is a little more complicated. You must first disable Postini before adding the domains in Google Apps, and then manage the new configuration directly from Postini. There are also several limitations in the way Postini manages multiple domains, the common theme being that domain aliases cannot have different configurations from the primary domain.

User Settings tab

By default, Google Apps shares contacts between the users of a domain, creating a global address book that all users can see. On this page, you can disable this behavior, so that contact lists are private to each user.

Appearance tab

Google Apps allows you to white-label the appearance of the Apps services by uploading your own logo and selecting from a range of color schemes for the sign-in page (or defining your own).

You can choose to replace the Google logo on each service home page with your own for your organization. In pixels, the graphic needs to be set to 143 wide by 59 high and saved in PNG or GIF format. Although you are allowed to use the phrase "Powered by Google", you're not allowed to use any other Google logos or trademarks, or any other copyrighted or illegal images. The logo will appear on your users page usually within an hour or so due to browsing caching, and will replace the Google logo in the top left.

The sign-in box color can be set to one of seven pre-defined schemes, or your own border and background colors (in hexadecimal).

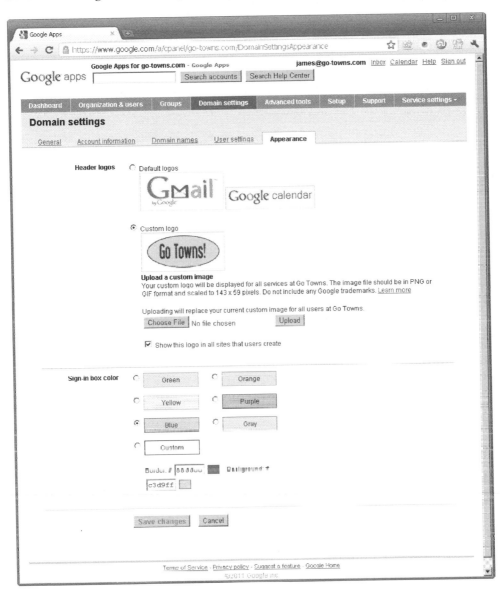

Setup & Support tabs

Google has recently added a setup wizard to assist new administrators in setting up their domains. Apart from providing step-by-step details for many common administrative tasks, there are also a range of educational tools and resources to help your users become accustomed to the platform. Additionally, the support tab contains useful links for administrators, end users and references to third party vendors.

Advanced Tools

Advanced tools is the fourth tab in the dashboard, and provides access to migration and integration features most often used by larger organizations.

The settings here fall into the following categories:

- **Migration**: the bulk user upload tool (shown earlier) and user email upload utilities. The first creates accounts and the second populates the inboxes with existing messages from legacy systems. The PC version of the email tool is available at **http://tools.google.com/dlpage/outlookmigration**.

- **Integration**: launcher icons for Google Apps services, installable directly to the Microsoft Windows desktop. These icons use the Google Chrome Browser to launch users into their Google Apps accounts, and create a more 'application-like' experience. You can install the icons by clicking the link (or distributing the URL to your users).

- **Security**: administrators can enable 2-factor authentication, meaning that a verification code is used in addition to the regular Google Apps password. This code is sent to the user's cell phone, and changes each time a new IP address is detected upon logging in. This prevents hackers in possession of guessed or stolen passwords from breaching the account as easily, and is similar to measures used in common online banking applications. Although administrators can enable the feature on a site-wide basis across a domain, users must choose to activate it individually.

- **Authentication**: since spammers can forge the "From" address in an email, you can use DomainKeys Identified Mail to help mail recipients confirm that your email really originated from your domain. Activating this feature involves adding a DNS TEXT record to your DNS settings, though this step is automatic if you purchased your domain name through Google Apps.

Most organizations implementing Google Apps find the user provisioning features in the Dashboard are adequate for managing users and defining access rights. But often larger companies look to automated solutions that are more fine-tuned to their needs, enabling the modification of large numbers of accounts without having to make changes on an individual basis.

Google Apps has a rich API for interacting with the underlying services, so it's trivial to create custom applications that automate tasks within Google applications. The API is compatible with a variety of structured languages, such as Java and .NET, while providing flexible integration with popular scripting languages such as PHP and Python.

This is where the Provisioning API comes into play and it's offered in all premier versions of Google Apps. A strong documentation base is available at **http://code.google.com/googleapps/domain/email_migration/developers_guide_ protocol.html**, and the site features an active developer forum to discuss ideas and problems.

Typically, any developer with a reasonable knowledge of scripting languages can build quite powerful and customized scripts within a short period of time by using these resources. Alternatively, there are many vendors in the Google Apps Marketplace who can either customize existing scripts or help with new API projects.

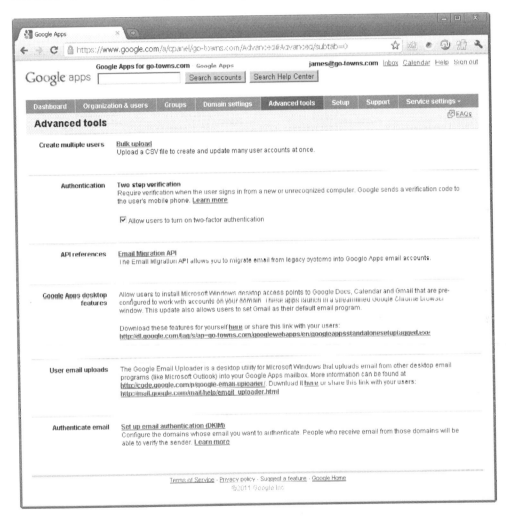

You can visit the Google Apps Marketplace at https://www.google.com/enterprise/marketplace.

Service Settings

The final tab in the dashboard contains service-level configuration features for each application within Google Apps. Click the **Service settings** dropdown to see your list of applications (these will vary depending on whether you use the Standard or Premier edition, and which apps Google has added since the publication of this book).

For each service, you have the option of changing the sub-domain URL (see Chapter 2) or disabling the service entirely. It's perfectly acceptable to use Google Apps for email and calendar, but not for Google Docs or Sites - or vice versa. Turning services on or off from this page affects all users in your domain.

Email settings

There are two important settings here:

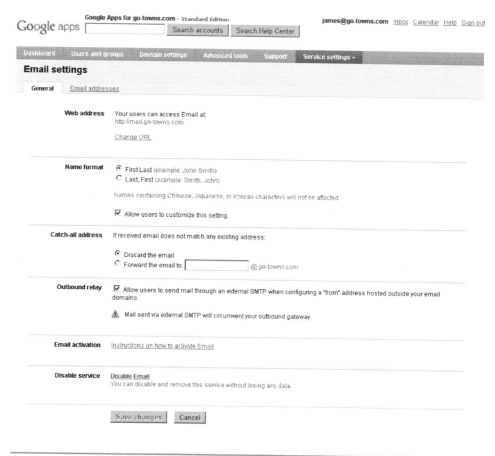

- **Catch-all addresses**: usually, *anything*@yourdomain.com will be bounced back to the sender, unless there is a mailbox with that name. This is the equivalent of sending a piece of mail to an invalid number at a valid street - the post office will return the mail. A catch-all is an alternative forwarding address used when a mailbox doesn't exist. Generally speaking, it's a good idea to create a catch-all, although it can increase the amount of spam the forwarding email receives.

- **Outbound relay**: by default, users can configure an external mail server in their Gmail account, which can circumvent Postini and your outbound gateway. For most organizations, this should be disabled.

Chat settings

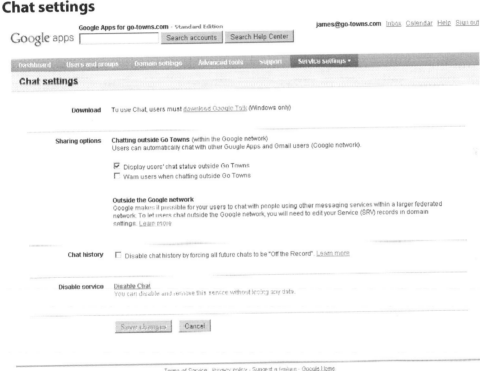

In configuring Google Chat, you have to decide if you want users to be able to communicate with Google users outside of your Apps domain. You have the choice of publishing your users' status externally, and warning users when chatting with people outside. You can also disable the chat history on a global level, so that none of your users' conversations is captured.

> The decisions you make here will largely be determined by your corporate I.T., communication and privacy policies.

Calendar settings

The calendar settings screen has two settings:

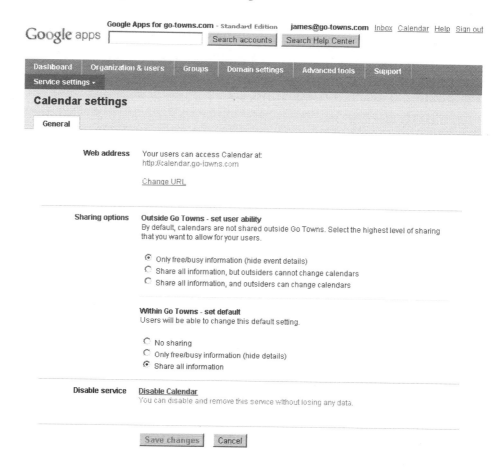

- **Sharing options ▶ Set user ability**: this sets the maximum visibility that's possible with calendars on your domain. The lowest level is the default, allowing viewers outside the domain to see only when time periods are free or busy, hiding the details of the appointment. The next level up gives outsiders a read-only view, while the most open state allows calendars to be writable externally. Owners of a calendar may still set permissions that are more restrictive.

- **Sharing options ▶ Set default**: users have a choice of three levels of security per calendar. The most restrictive makes a calendar private only to that user (and those individuals they explicitly share it with), the next level up shares only when the calendar is free or busy, and the least restrictive shares all the information on the calendar. The option you select here will set the default level of visibility, although users can still override this choice.

Docs settings

The Docs settings screen has two similar options:

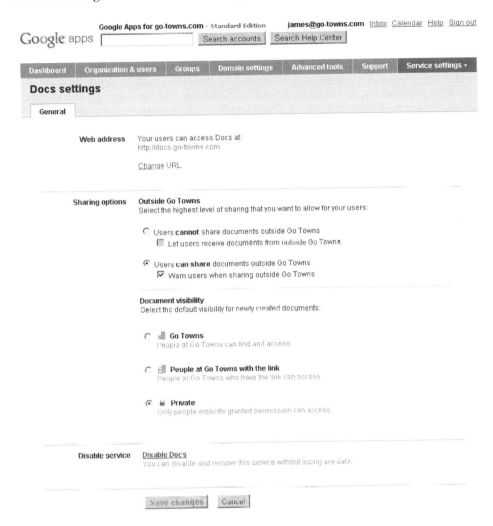

- **Sharing options ▶ Outside domain**: this global setting determines if users can share documents with those outside the domain. If you disable this, you still have the option to enable users to receive documents from outsiders. If you enable the feature, you can also warn the user whenever they share outside the domain.

- **Sharing options ▶ Document visibility**: by default, newly-created documents are only visible to the creator. With this setting, you can increase the visibility to either only people who have the link, or everyone on the domain. The user still has the option to override the default setting when they create the document.

Sites settings

There are two settings available from this screen:

- **General ▶ Sharing options**: this global setting defines the maximum level of visibility available to sites created by users on your domain. Users may still select a level that's more restrictive than what is defined here. The options are to stop external sharing completely, allow it for specific external users (with or without a warning), or to make a site publicly readable.

- **Web address mapping ▶ Add a new web address**: this is covered in more detail in Chapter 2, but essentially allows you to replace the default site address with an address on your domain. This means the URL will be shortened from **http://sites.google.com/a/yourdomain.com/site-name** to **http://site-name. yourdomain.com**. Generally speaking, this is something you will want to do for every production site in your domain.

- **Web address mapping ▶ Delete mapping(s)**: here you can remove any existing mappings by selecting the web address and clicking **Delete mapping(s)**.

Mobile settings

The screen provides the following help for setting up mobile users on your domain:

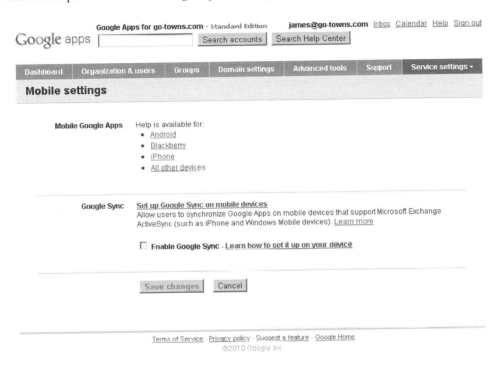

If you plan on using mobile devices with your Google Apps domain, this page provides information on how to set up access depending upon your platform. Many Google Apps are installed natively on Android devices so that you only need to sign-in on the phone to synchronize your account. For the Apple iPhone, apps need to be downloaded from the App Store, and for Blackberry users, visiting **http://m.google.com** from the phone's browser will take you to the most current range of apps available.

Since mobile platforms are developing rapidly and there are many other types of phone that can connect to Google Apps, I would recommend reading the help information provided here for your specific platform to see the most up-to-date way to connect. The key part of this screen is the option **Enable Google Sync**, which must be checked if you want your users to access their accounts through mobile devices.

Google Apps Premier and Educational Editions have addition options to enforce a minimum level of encryption on a mobile device and to enforce a password policy, so that a strong password is required to view Google Apps data. Additionally, it's possible to reset a user's password and to remotely wipe a device of all its data, in case the phone is lost or stolen.

Checking for Google Apps outages

If you discover that you can't access one of the Google Apps services, Google provides the Apps Status Dashboard, available at **http://www.google.com/appsstatus**. The page is the official hub for any problems with the services, showing current and historical outages. You can also use the page's RSS feed in any RSS reader.

The dashboard shows the current state of all major services using the following icons:

- **Green tick**: no issues.

- **Yellow wrench**: there are issues affecting a subset of users.

- **Red cross**: a complete service outage.

- **Information icon**: provides follow-up information for a previous interruption in service, after the resolution of the outage.

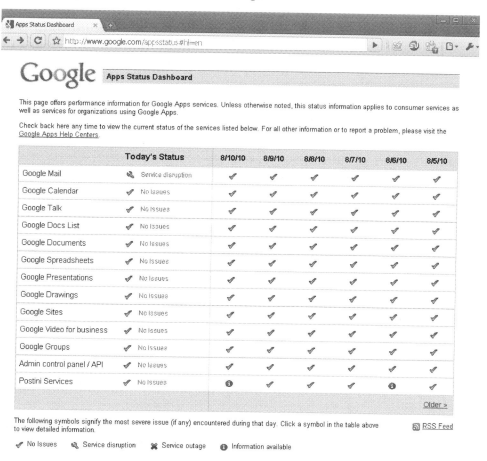

4: Gmail

While there are clear limitations in some of the Google Apps services, since they generally provide only a subset of features of their Microsoft Office equivalents, I believe Gmail is the one application that stands head and shoulders above any other free or paid email software. Gmail combines a fast, intuitive interface that's extremely quick to learn with all the major benefits of working in the cloud: you can store and search gigabytes of messages seamlessly and access your email anywhere.

It also boasts an intelligent spam filtering technology, with many companies reporting a substantial drop in the amount of spam that reaches end users, and simplifying the need for email blacklists and whitelists. Google Apps Premier users can modify the Postini configuration to tweak this spam filter with finer granularity. Additionally, file attachments in email are automatically scanned for viruses - although this can never be completely foolproof, it undoubtedly reduces the number of virus outbreaks on the desktop.

For mobile users, Gmail synchronizes seamlessly with many modern smartphones, and is integrated natively into Android devices, with apps available for iPhone and Blackberry. On top of all this, die-hard Microsoft Outlook users are still able to access their email through their preferred client, while taking advantage of Gmail's strengths running on the server side, which I consider superior to any Microsoft Exchange server implementation I've seen.

To get started with Gmail, once you have created a Google Apps account (see chapter 2), you can access it by opening a browser and visiting either:

- **http://mail.yourdomain.com**: if you set a custom URL for the service, you can access the site on your own sub-domain.

- **http://mail.google.com/a/yourdomain.com**: this is the default URL, which will always work even if you've set up a shortcut sub-domain.

In either case, you need to substitute *yourdomain.com* for whatever domain you registered or purchased in chapter 2. The first method is recommended purely because it's easier to remember, but they both lead to the same place.

If you use Gmail for personal use, you'll notice the different URL, since you may be used to visiting **http://mail.google.com** or **http://gmail.com**. You cannot log into your Google Apps accounts from these URLs because they are reserved for users of the free Gmail service, all of which have usernames that end in @gmail.com (or other Google extensions outside of the US).

The Basics

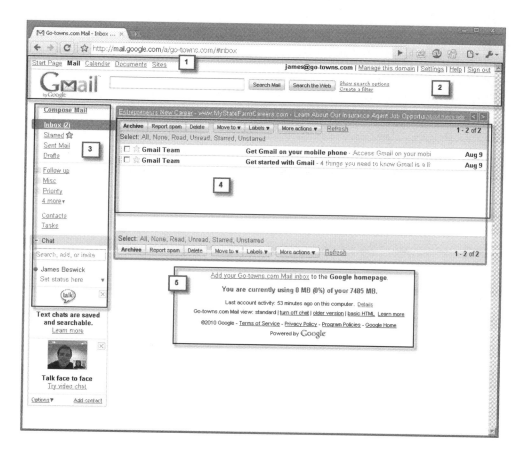

The standard view is composed of 5 general areas:

1. **Header left**: the most commonly used parts of Google Apps are shown as shortcuts in the top left.

2. **Header right**: settings, account management and help and shown on the right. The search area enables you to search all your messages or the web.

3. **Folders**: the left-hand tabs split the messages into their different states (inbox, draft, outbox, trash, etc.), as well as showing spam and starred messages. This is also where labels and other widgets are shown, as we'll see later.

4. **Messages**: displays the messages in the selected folder, as well as a snippet of the message, any labels and a timestamp.

5. **Footer**: this shows your quota usage, enables session changes, together with a security feature showing IP addresses that are logged into your account.

Writing email

Clicking **Compose Mail** displays this screen:

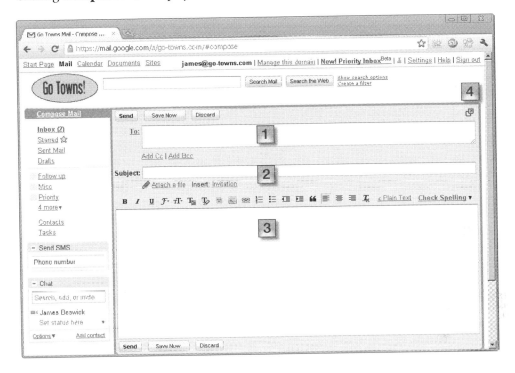

The key areas are:

1. **To/Cc/Bcc**: these fields assist you in selecting email addresses already known to Gmail, or you can add lists of emails separated by commas or semi-colons. Any email address you use will be stored in your contacts list.

2. **Extras**: these sections expand if you use them and consist of:

   - **File attachments**: click to add a file. While you type the rest of the message, the file will be uploaded in the background. If you decide not to send the file after all, just uncheck the selection box.

   - **Event**: you can choose to add event details to the email, which will automatically be added to your default calendar.

3. **Message area**: this is where you enter the body of your email.

4. **Undock icon**: to work on a message in its own window, click here. This separates the email from the main display, and can help users of Microsoft Outlook feel more comfortable with the interface.

When you create emails, Gmail supports plain text, marked-up text (bold, italic, etc), tables and images. Your messages can be formatted using the toolbox options, and Gmail also supports complex marked-up HTML in messages (you can paste entire web-pages into a message, for example). The spell check auto-detects the language and also has dictionaries for dozens of additional languages

You can also attach signatures, files and appointments, and select your recipients in three fields:

- **To**: the primary recipient(s).

- **CC**: meaning 'carbon copy', the message reaches the recipients in exactly the same way, but tends to indicate to people in this field that they are not the primary readers.

- **BCC**: meaning 'blind carbon copy', this hides the names and email addresses of listed recipients (useful for mass emails or when you don't want recipients to know each other).

As you complete these fields, Gmail will match each name against your Contacts list as you type (press **Tab** or **Enter** to confirm a match):

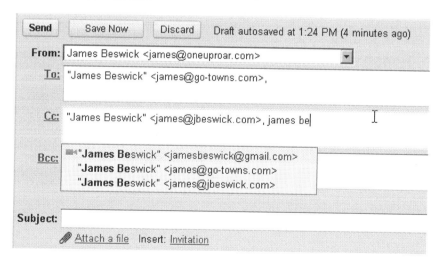

The Contacts list consists of people who belong to your address book, and those you have received email from previously. If you want to add multiple entries in any the To, CC or BCC fields, separate these with a comma or semi-colon.

Gmail continuously saves your message every few seconds, so even if you navigate to another page before sending, it will appear in the Drafts folder. Once you have composed your opus, click **Send**.

Reading email

Back in the messages view, clicking any email will open its contents. The menu options are the same, except for a drop-down on the top right, shown below:

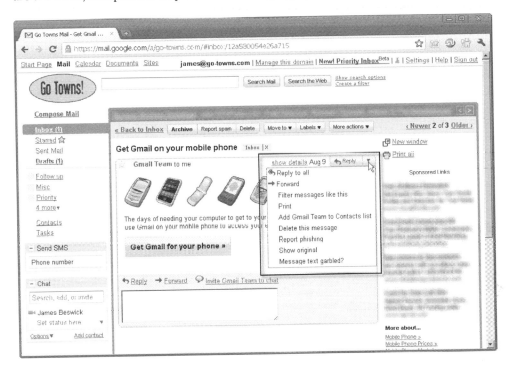

This dropdown repeats some of the options elsewhere on the page but also contains some of the less-frequently used features:

- **Filter messages like these**: we'll cover filtering shortly - this option is an easy way to create a filter based upon who sent the current message.

- **Print**: this is the same as **Print All** on the right, and will reformat the message (and remove visual navigation features) to make the email more printer-friendly.

- **Report Phishing**: phishing emails are ones that appear to be sent from a legitimate source, such as online auctions or banks, requesting personal information with the objective of illegally accessing your account. If you receive these, reporting the messages to Google will help remove the same messages from other users' mailboxes (since they are usually sent to large numbers of users).

- **Show original**: Gmail renders any HTML in the email, but this option allows you to see the original text, including message headers.

- **Message text garbled?** If the email contains characters unsupported by your default text encoding, switch to an encoding more appropriate for the language.

At the end of the message, click **Reply**, **Forward** or anywhere in the white box to open the Compose Mail screen (which is added to the bottom of the existing thread). As recipients reply to each other, messages stack up with the most recent part of the thread appearing at the bottom. Gmail will also collapse older messages to make it easier to see newer ones, and you can expand these by clicking the header.

Message threading is one of the most useful features of Gmail, because it logically handles emails bouncing between several members of a group. Whereas other email clients treat each reply as a separate message, Gmail realizes they're part of a conversation and organizes them appropriately.

There are two options that are particularly handy if an email is popular and many recipients are responding rapidly:

- **New message alert** (see below): if any recipient responds while you are either viewing or typing a reply, you will receive a notification, giving you the opportunity to change your reply.

- **Mute**: under the **More Actions** menu, Mute tells Gmail to ignore any further updates on this particular email thread. This eliminates the so-called 'mail storm' problem that can occur.

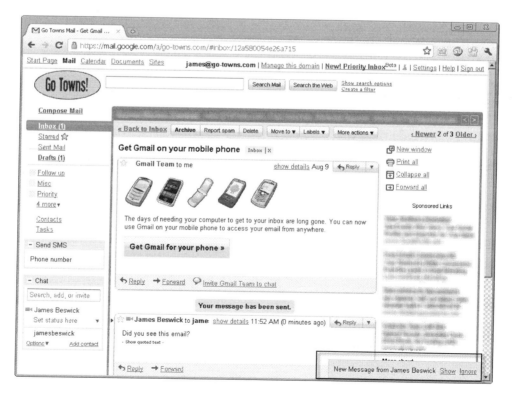

Configuration options

The navigation of Gmail is simple – reading and writing messages represent the most common user operations, so the focus on making this easy is one of the reasons why Gmail is so popular. But simple doesn't mean basic, and there are many ways to fine-tune its functionality.

User settings are located in the **Settings** hyperlink in the top right of the page. Options are split logically into tab groupings, and we will review the key tabs and features here. Depending on whether you are using just Gmail alone or as part of Google Apps, the options will vary slightly.

Since Google frequently adds and changes features and options, these configuration pages are getting ever more numerous and complicated. The upside is that you can really fine tune its performance to exactly what you want, though at the expense of finding settings quickly and sometimes having to decipher what they mean.

General tab

- **Language**: select your primary language (US English by default).

- **Maximum page size**: how many emails appear per page (the display is faster when set to 25 and slower when set to 100).

- **Keyboard shortcuts**: a complete list of shortcuts is available at **http://mail.google.com/support/bin/answer.py?hl=en&answer=6594**, and these can be toggled on and off.

- **External content**: by default, Gmail doesn't display images in emails from 'untrusted' sources. This prevents senders from detecting that you have read the message. Once a sender becomes trusted, Gmail relaxes this setting, but you can forcibly prevent any images from automatically loading using this setting.

- **Browser connection**: you can choose to force HTTPS, so traffic between your browser and Gmail servers is secure. There's a small performance loss due to encryption but in almost every case this should be enabled. Note that even if you disable secure traffic, the Google login screen is always encrypted to protect your username and password.

- **Conversation view**: Gmail threads messages so responses between recipients appear as a conversation. If you are used to other email systems that don't do this, you have the option to disable threading here.

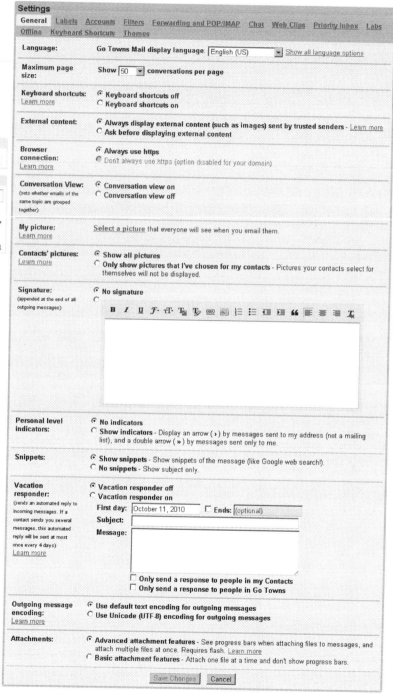

- **Language**: select your primary language (US English by default).

- **My picture**: a profile picture visible to other Gmail users. This picture will appear anywhere your Google profile is available, including Android phones, though you can modify the privacy setting so only contacts can see it.

- **Contacts pictures**: here you can choose whether you can see other Google users' pictures - by default, this is enabled.

- **Signature**: this is text that appears at the end of each email (typically the sender's contact information). It can be formatted using the standard text editor and may include images and links. If you have multiple email aliases, you can set a different signature for each alias.

- **Personal level indicators**: shows a › symbol before emails sent specifically to you, and » for those sent only to you, which helps weeding out bulk emails.

- **Show snippets**: display a line of text from each message in the message view to indicate content, enabled by default.

- **Vacation response**: sends an automated reply to incoming mail, most often used for vacation messages but can also be used to generate any type of automatic acknowledgement.

- **Outgoing message encoding**: leave the default setting here, unless you have a specific reason to change it (specifically, if you are not able to read your messages, switch to UTF-8).

- **Attachments**: choose between the advanced and basic attachment feature. The advanced version allows you to add multiple files simultaneously and shows a progress bar for uploading - but it requires Adobe Flash. If you have problems with Flash or simply don't want to use it, switch to the basic version.

Labels tab

Labels can be tricky to explain to new users, although they are Gmail's primary method of organization. Unlike most other email services, Gmail doesn't have a folder-based filing system and relies on labels instead. Labels are like tags, so any given email can have one or more labels, but the labels aren't nested in the same way that folders are.

Once you get used to labels, it becomes a more natural way to store and find messages, since email is largely unstructured and informal data. I use labels such as Travel, Receipts, Work and San Francisco (where I live), and since I can apply more than one label to each email, frequently I will use combinations (e.g. Travel and Receipts for an airline booking or Work and San Francisco for jobs located there).

This may not seem particularly clever, but in the world of folders, this wouldn't be possible since one email can belong to only one folder. So I would probably end up duplicating sub-folders (e.g. a Receipts folder in each of the Personal and Work parent folders). But I think the labels concept enables a more flexible organizational strategy for my email.

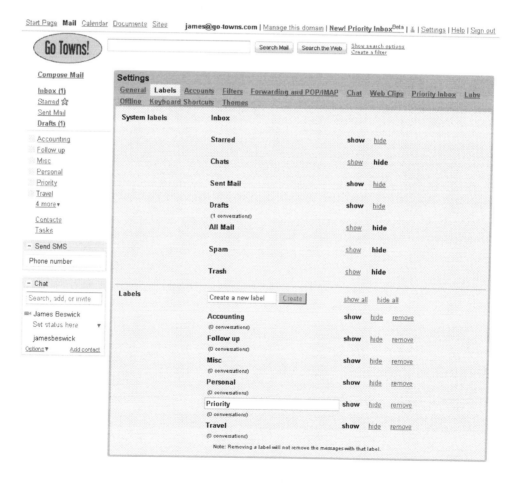

The labels tab is the central place to manage labels, although you can also carry out many of the functions where the labels are stacked on the left-hand side. Gmail provides some system-level and custom labels by default, which are shown when the tab is selected.

System labels are at the core of how Gmail manages the flow of email, and it's worth digging into this functionality a little. When an email arrives, it's automatically given the Inbox label, and when you click the Inbox link, you are essentially filtering for messages that have that label. When you archive an email, this removes the Inbox label but actually does nothing else. Consequently, archiving doesn't have any effect other than stripping the inbox label.

The same is true for deletion - when you delete an email, it removes the Inbox label and adds the Trash label. And yes, that works for spam too - an email marked as spam simply attracts the spam label (and removes the Inbox label). I'm laboring this point since it's different to conventional email which physically moves the messages from one place to another - in Gmail, the message never moves, it just changes labels.

Back to system labels, these can only be hidden or shown - with the exception of the Inbox which, not too surprisingly, must always be shown. Hiding a label doesn't delete it - it only removes the shortcut on the left-side navigation. If you never check spam messages or the trash, hiding these labels saves screen real estate.

The only system label that's a little different is All Mail, which is applied to every message you ever send or receive. Enabling this label creates a view of every inbound and outbound message, ordered chronologically, only excluding those in Trash or Spam. The All Mail view is hidden by default.

In addition to system labels, you can create (and delete) custom labels, which will appear on the left side navigation in alphabetical order. Deleting a label doesn't remove any messages tagged with that label. Custom labels can have a maximum length of 40 characters.

Although I've pitched labels as an alternative to nested folders, if you *really* want to use nesting, there's a Google Labs feature that will do this called Nested Labels. If you enable this feature then you can use a forward-slash to show structure. For example, the three labels "Budget/2009", "Budget/2010" and "Budget/2011" would expand out of a fourth label "Budget" as shown below. This gives the impression of a folder structure, which definitely helps some users organizationally. We'll be covering Gmail's Labs features in more detail later.

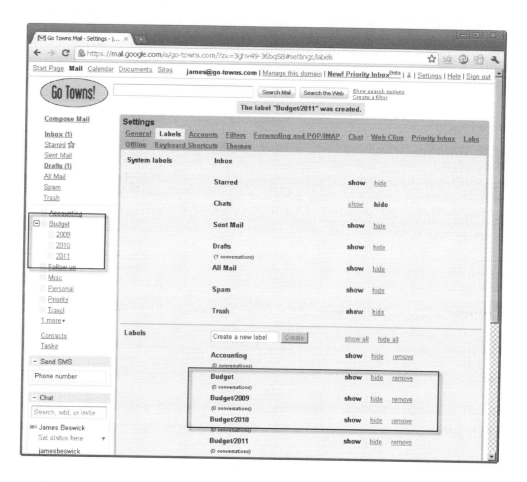

Finally, you can add color-coding to labels by clicking the arrow that appears when hovering over the left-hand menu. There are a range of default colors, or you can select a custom color:

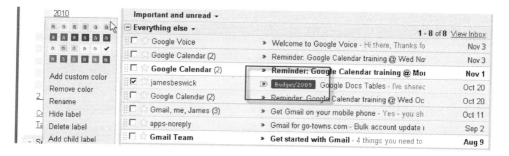

Once a color is applied to a label, any messages with that label will inherit the color. While this feature can make messages easier to locate quickly, it tends to work best when colors are not applied to every label. From the same drop-down menu, you can also remove the color, hide or delete the label, or add a sub-label.

Accounts tab

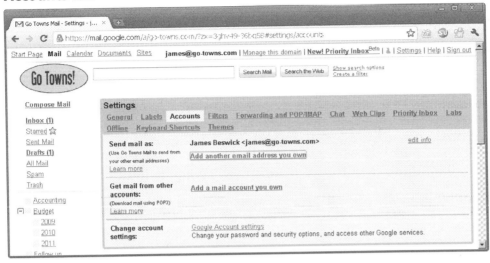

There are two useful features here, both frequently overlooked.

Send mail as modifies your outgoing email address (e.g. james@somedomain.com instead of james@go-towns.com), so that your message appears to come from another account. To prevent abuse, you have to verify that you have access to that account, which simply means clicking a link in a verification email sent to the alias. It's important to realize that this only changes the "From" address on your email, and mail sent to the alias will still be delivered to whichever service handles that address.

When you activate this feature, a new field called **From** appears when you compose or reply to mail. This is a drop-down of all your available account names. Additionally, the Signature section under the **General** tab will also let you add multiple signatures (one for each confirmed alias).

Get mail from other accounts allows you to set up mail retrieval from other systems supporting POP3, so Gmail can retrieve email for up to 5 other accounts and become your central email application. Clicking the option provides detailed setup instructions based upon which third-party email provider you are using. The service is called Mail Fetcher, and will periodically check for new messages for accounts you define.

> In the regular non-Apps version of Gmail, there is also an import option on this screen which assists with bringing mail from Yahoo!, Hotmail and other POP3 accounts into Gmail. This option does not appear in the Google Apps version.

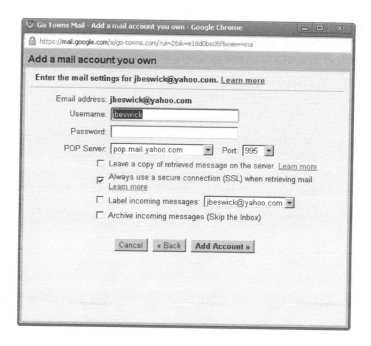

When you enter the third-party email address, Gmail will auto-complete the server settings for the most popular providers. If the POP Server and Port fields are not automatically filled in, check with your email provider to confirm their settings. In addition to the Username and Password fields, you have 4 other settings:

- **Leave a copy of retrieved messages on the server**: if this is checked, messages will be retained on the third-party email service. If unchecked, they will be deleted after they are imported to Gmail.

- **Always use a secure connection (SSL) when retrieving mail**: if the third-party service supports SSL, it's advisable to leave this checked for security reasons. You will receive an error if this option is checked and it's not supported by the third-party.

- **Label incoming messages**: you can automatically add a label to incoming messages from other accounts, which may help you identify which account they belong to.

- **Archive incoming messages (Skip the Inbox)**: by default, new messages from the third-party account are treated the same way as new messages in Gmail. Checking this option overrides that behavior and immediately archives all new messages.

The final option on the Accounts tab provides a link to your Google Accounts option, which affects all other Google services outside of Gmail.

Filters tab

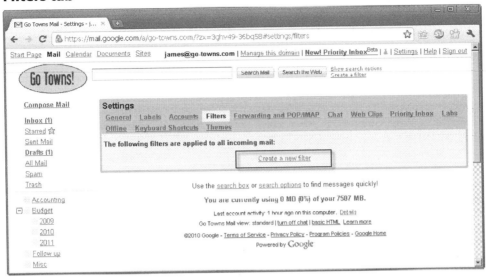

I receive around 400-500 emails a day and filters allow me to work out which ones I should read, those I should just archive - and those I can just delete! Filters are the Gmail equivalent of mailbox rules – incoming messages are tested against predefined conditions and action is taken accordingly. This may sound complicated, but it really helps manage the email tsunami that would otherwise make the entire system almost unusable.

You can use filters to automatically label, archive, delete or forward emails, based upon one or more criteria. This creates an automated action that would otherwise be manual. There are two ways to create a filter, the most common being to click **Create Filter** next to the search box or **Create a new filter** in the Filters tab.

The filter can monitor messages from a particularly sender, to a particular recipient, or containing specific keywords in the subject or body (you can also test for attachments or the absence of certain keywords).

Once you have defined the rules, click **Test Search** to show which messages in your mailbox would have been affected historically, in order to check the logic of the filter. If the results are as expected, click **Next Step** to define the action taken.

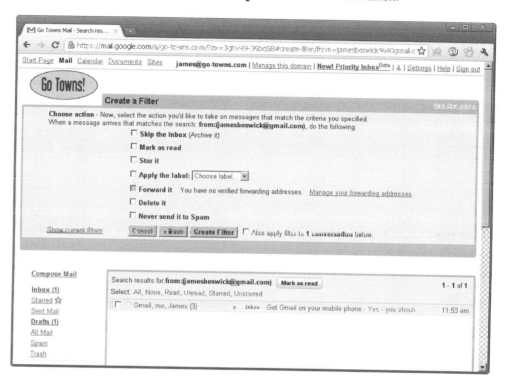

Here you define the required action. For example:

- Forward any email with the word 'Sales' to the entire sales group for immediate attention.

- Ensure a daily newsletter is never marked as spam.

- Automatically add a star or label to every message from a particular sender.

For example, I receive an email from Twitter every time somebody follows my account, and I can identify these messages by using these criteria:

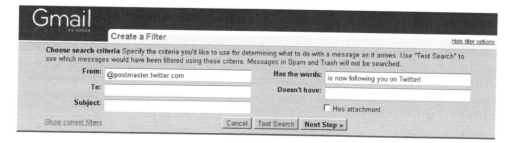

In this example the address "@postmaster.twitter.com" indicates that the filter applies to any sender from this domain. In the next step, I then check **Skip the Inbox** and choose my Twitter label under **Apply the label** - these messages are now neatly filed under the correct label and never directly reach my inbox.

Rather than creating a filter from scratch, you can also create one while viewing an email, and the settings will be auto-filled based upon that message. While viewing a message, click the **More Actions** drop-down and select **Filter messages like these**. Gmail then completes the From field, otherwise the process is identical.

Once filters are created, they can be edited or deleted from the Filters tab in the **Settings** menu. Click the edit or delete link next to the filter you want to change: editing shows the familiar set of filter options, and delete immediately removes the filter (unfortunately there's no confirmation or undo option).

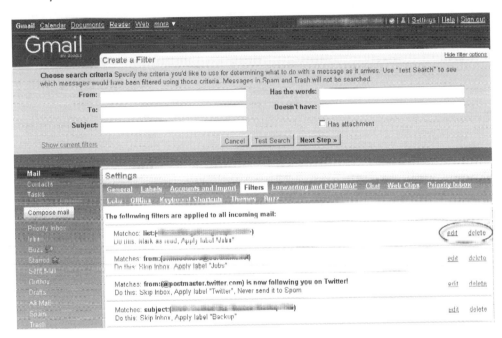

If you discover that filters are not performing as expected - for example, messages that should be filtered are not - double check your parameters to ensure you are not:

- **Over-restrictive**: too many parameters try to identify messages too precisely.

- **Over-broad**: parameters are too general, and cause too many messages to match the filter.

If you find a filter used to work and then stops, check the messages to see what has changed (e.g. bulk emails often change their sender address and defeat filters).

Forwarding and POP/IMAP

Since you may have more than one email address, you might find it convenient to have Gmail messages forwarded to another account, or managed from another email program entirely.

Why would you do this when Gmail is so easy to use?

- **Familiarity**: many users are comfortable with their existing desktop email client, such as Microsoft Outlook, and can be resistant to moving to another application.

- **Missing features**: some users may rely on features available in their email client but simply not available in Gmail (or the user isn't aware of the feature).

- **Policies**: larger corporations may have I.T. and compliance policies that require the use of certain software or prohibit browser-based applications. Companies in this position can still use Gmail servers and an alternative front-end, and their users will be unaware of the hybrid setup.

In any case, Gmail can be configured to work with most popular email clients, so these users have the benefits of Gmail storage and remote access while also working in their preferred email program.

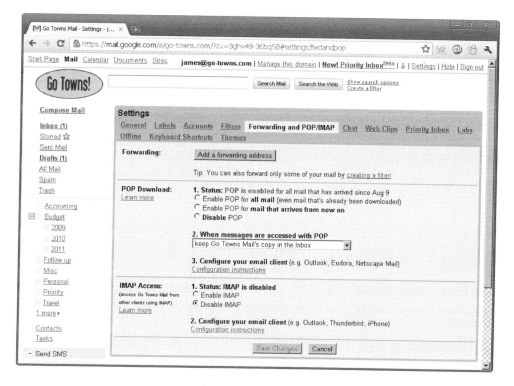

To forward messages, you have to specify two settings:

- **Email address**: the destination where the email should go.

- **Action**: delete the forwarded mail from Gmail, archive it, or leave it unread.

Using the forwarding method sends everything that arrives to your Gmail address to your selected third party. But wait - doesn't this look a little like a filter? Indeed it is, and you can also use a filter to achieve exactly the same result, but with a filter you could be even more specific and forward only a portion of your email.

Setting up POP and IMAP (which are two different protocols for communicating with mail servers) is a little more involved. From an administrative point-of-view, IMAP generally causes fewer problems since it uses two-way communication which makes integration more transparent with Gmail. If you have a choice of protocol, IMAP *should* provide a more stable experience.

With POP, you have a choice of enabling access to all mail historically or all mail from this point forward. Depending upon the mail client and the user requirements, it's often more stable to restrict POP access only to mail that arrives from now on. If the Gmail account has gigabytes of emails already, many external clients don't handle very large mailboxes gracefully. If you are responsible for managing this integration, I would suggest testing thoroughly to ensure a stable user experience.

Whichever protocol you choose (and you can choose both, though it's not recommended), click the associated **Configuration Instructions** hyperlink. As this is the most complex part to set up, Google Help has detailed information on the exact steps with all the major mail clients.

From an administrative standpoint, it's preferable to avoid time-consuming Outlook-to-Gmail setups, simply because the zero-installation nature of Gmail is one of the benefits of using it in the first place. There are also some other unexpected side-effects:

- The threaded conversations will become separated, and depending on your label usage may be duplicated several times in your email client.

- Certain views in Gmail are not available (such as Chat).

- The speed of searching will often be much slower on a local email client (especially with large mailboxes), compared with the lightning search capabilities of server-based Gmail.

Chat tab

Chat is the instant messaging component of Gmail, but unlike email can include video and audio in addition to text. Also unlike email, you will need to install a plug-in for the full functionality, available at **http://www.google.com/chat/video**. Once this is downloaded and installed, restart your browser and then visit the **Chat** tab in Settings:

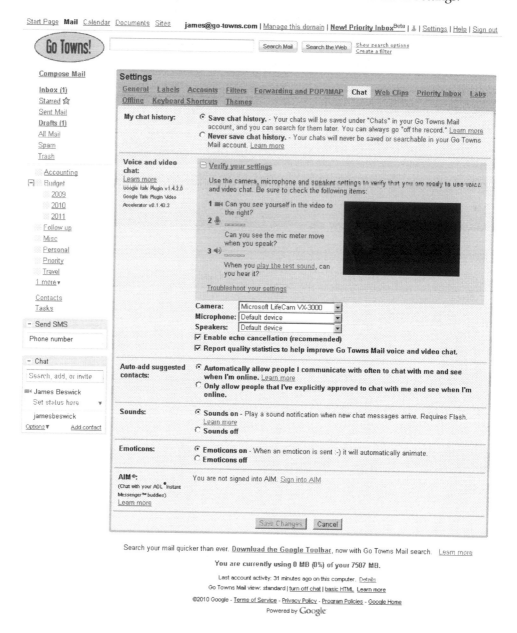

- **My chat history**: you can choose to have your chats stored like email, so they will appear whenever the Chats label is clicked and they will also appear in search results. If you don't want every chat to be recorded this way, you can choose to go 'Off the Record' for any individual chat session. If you don't want anything stored, simply check the option to disable the history.

- **Voice and video chat**: once you have installed the Google Talk plugin, modify the settings here to ensure that your video and audio are working as expected. Google Talk should configure your default devices correctly, but it's worth double-checking before your first call. You should not disable echo cancellation unless you're specifically experiencing problems with its performance.

- **Call Phones**: if you have signed up for a free Google Voice account, enabling this feature will allow you to place calls directly from Gmail, using the Google Voice number as the outgoing caller ID. If you do not have a Google Voice account, the caller ID seen by the recipient will be generic.

- **Auto-add suggested contacts**: as you use Google Apps, the system will automatically create a list of contacts for the Chat application. This usually works without any issues, but if you're concerned about privacy, you can override this feature and enforce the explicit approval for each new contact entry.

- **Sounds**: by default - and if you have Flash - Chat will play an audio alert whenever a new conversation is started (or a new message arrives and you're doing something else on your computer).

- **Emoticons**: Gmail will convert text-based emotions (such as :-D) into animated equivalents. Since the range of emoticons has become somewhat elaborate over the years, it makes sense to leave this enabled unless you're well-versed.

- **AIM**: if you use AOL's Instant Messenger tool, you can set up Chat to use it through OpenAIM

Once enabled, the Chat panel appears under the label list on the left and contains:

- **Status options**: by default, Google shows your presence as 'Available' whenever you are on Gmail. You can override this with a custom message, show yourself as busy, or become invisible to other contacts.

- **Contacts**: Google determines the people you most frequently communicate with and adds them to this list. You can toggle between this 'Most popular' list or 'All contacts'.

- **Call phone**: Gmail allows free calls to US land lines and cell phones, though only for US-based users as of 2011. There are also discounted international rates available from the same interface.

Web Clips tab

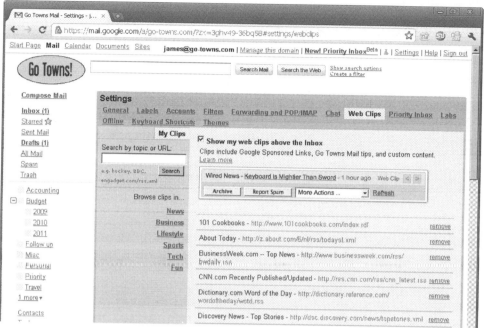

At the top of the messages view, there's a single line that rotates occasionally featuring an external link that's hopefully of interest – these can be configured or disabled here. The categories on the left lead to a wide range of feeds, so you can specify your interests and let Google keep you entertained.

To remove individual feeds - and there are many enabled by default - click **My Clips** and then click the corresponding **Remove link**. If you want to completely remove web-clips, uncheck the **Show my web clips** option at the top.

Beyond the standard public feeds covering everything from news and weather to technology and sports, you can search by topic (e.g. "DVD releases") or add a URL for any RSS feed. This can be useful in company situations, since you can publish corporate news automatically as Web Clips just by creating an RSS feed and providing the address to your users.

As another example, it's easy to add a Twitter timeline to the web clips, just by finding the RSS link on any public Twitter profile. My Twitter RSS link is **http://twitter.com/statuses/user_timeline/113146460.rss** and pasting this as a new feed causes my Tweets to rotate in the web clips (it can take a few hours to start appearing).

Priority Inbox

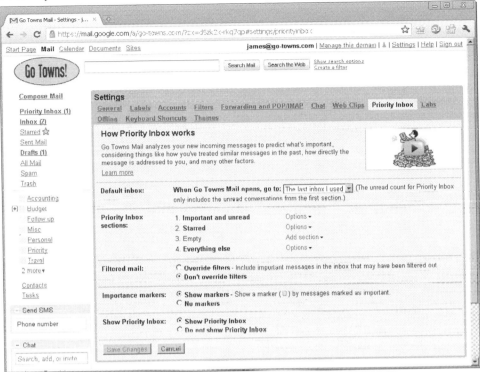

Priority Inbox is a newer feature of Gmail that aims to analyze your incoming messages to determine those that are the most important to you. Based upon actions you've taken in the past, Gmail learns how to prioritize new messages. You can configure how the Priority Inbox works here:

- **Default Inbox**: choose whether Gmail displays the regular Inbox or the Priority Inbox when you first open Gmail.

- **Priority Inbox sections**: there are up to four sections, all of which can be personalized based upon whether messages are starred, important, read or unread by clicking the **Options** hyperlink. You can also use a section to show only messages with a certain label, and you can set how many messages can appear in each part.

- **Filtered mail**: normally, Priority Inbox checks your filters first, so if a filter sends a mail to the Trash or archives it immediately, the behavior remains the same. You can choose to ignore filters and allow Priority Inbox to assess every incoming messages regardless of your filters.

- **Show Priority Inbox**: the feature can be completely enabled or disabled here.

Google Labs tab

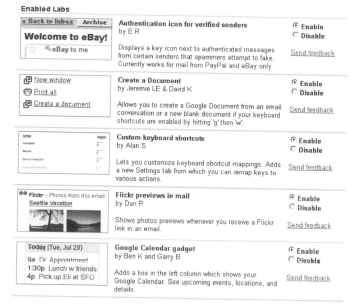

Google develops experimental features rapidly and allows willing users to participate in projects that may not be ready for stable release in the form. This feature is called Labs and is available across all Google Apps editions, although the option to universally disable it is only available in the Business and Educational versions.

The implied contract with Labs features is that you can take part as a beta tester, but there are no guarantees they won't change, break or disappear without notice. On the flip side you can provide feedback and criticism directly to the development team, and take part in the community that discusses these potential upgrades.

Once a Labs feature has been tested and adopted by the user base, sometimes it's migrated to the regular platform. To access Labs, simply click on the green flask next to **Settings**, or find the Labs tab in the Settings menu. Labs items change frequently, but they broadly fall into three categories:

- **Fun ideas**: games, tweaks and sometimes downright bizarre options.

- **Visual enhancements**: themes, movable widgets, and layout changes.

- **Extensions**: SMS messaging, information from other Google Apps (e.g. Calendar, Docs, etc.), and new tools (e.g. task lists).

Each feature can be enabled or disabled by clicking the appropriate option next to its description. If a feature breaks or disables Gmail, you can access a 'safe mode' where Labs is turned off at **https://mail.google.com/mail/?labs=0**.

Offline tab

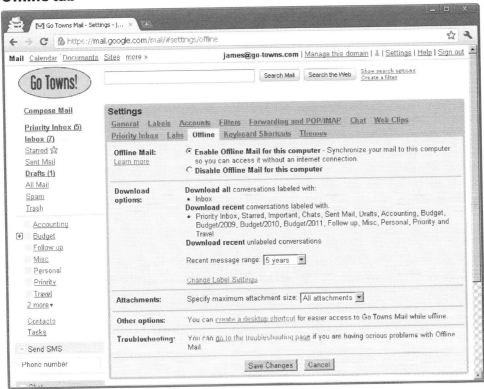

Offline access helps solve one of the biggest problems with browser-based software, namely that it usually stops working when you don't have Internet access. If you're frequently working on a plane or in other situations where the web is unavailable, Gmail would not have been a viable email client for you until offline was released.

Programs such as Microsoft Outlook continue to work offline because they cache messages locally on your computer and then synchronize when the Internet is available. Gmail Offline does exactly the same thing, although you will need to install a small piece of software called Google Gears, and allow it time to cache your mailbox first.

To get started with Offline:

1. Click **Enable Offline Mail for this computer** and then click **Save Changes**.

2. You will see a warning advising you not to enable offline for public or shared computers (see below). You should only use offline for your private desktop or laptop - proceed if this is the case.

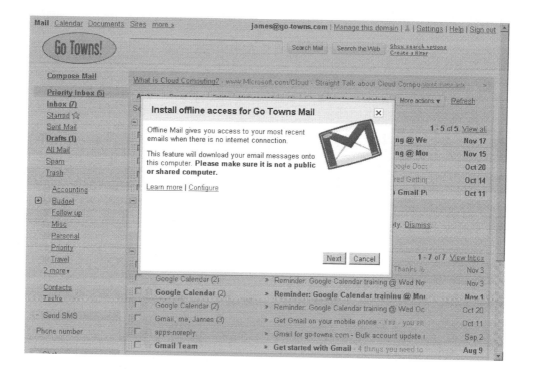

3. The next dialog box enables the installation of Google Gears and allows you to create shortcuts on your desktop (or start menu or launch bar). These shortcuts points your preferred browser to the offline Gmail application directly.

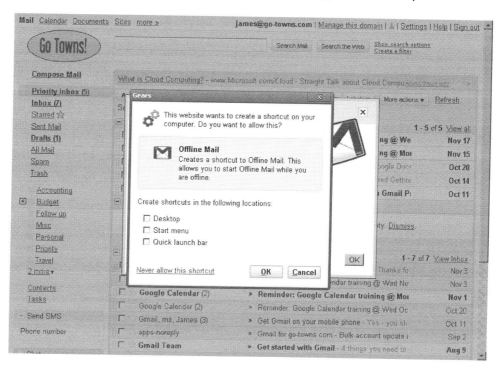

Back in the Offline settings tab, there are some options to fine-tune how the offline synchronization work:

- **Enable/Disable Offline**: this is where you can turn offline on or off.

- **Download options**: over time and usage, Gmail will decide which labels should be downloaded - it will choose to download everything or just recent messages. Unless you're frequently missing messages, you should let Gmail manage these settings. Click **Change Label Settings** to make changes to how different labels are treated.

- **Recent message range**: you can set the period from 4 days to 5 years. However, if you have a very large inbox, it can take hours to download messages if the range is too large. Again, Gmail's default is usually the best option to balance message availability and performance.

- **Attachments**: Offline will download any message attachments, but if you frequently receive large attachments and experience performance problems, limit the maximum size here.

Once Gmail Offline is enabled, you will see a new green icon in the header next to the Labs icon (if enabled). Click the icon to show the status of Gmail Offline, and a range of other options:

Most of the time, you will see a green tick indicating that synchronization is working without any problems. But if you have a poor Internet connection, or you have been working without a connection, there are two useful options:

- **Sync now**: Gmail will automatically re-sync when it finds a connection, but you can force it to do so from here. The major reason to use this is if an intermittent connection is causing the automatic synchronization to behave unreliably.

- **Go into Flaky Connection Mode**: this makes Gmail operate from your local cache and manages synchronizing in the background, assuming there's a poor connection.

Keyboard Shortcuts tab

For power users (and people familiar with command-line systems), Gmail's shortcuts make it one of the fastest email clients available. The major benefit is that you can avoid using the mouse for navigation, so repetitive tasks such as moving forward and backward through messages become easier.

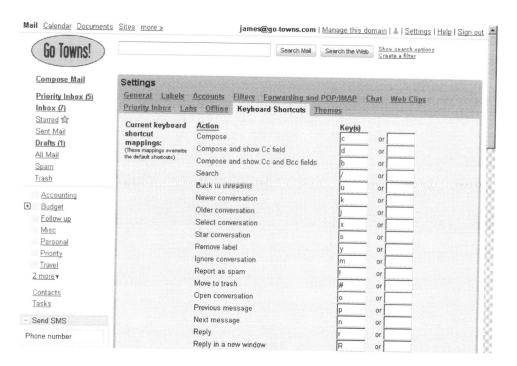

Every major function has a corresponding shortcut, and once you become proficient it's remarkable how quickly you can navigate the interface. Shortcuts are either one or two characters and many cannot be used when editing a message.

With shortcuts:

- You must first enable shortcuts from the **General** tab, since they are disabled by default (this is to prevent confusing new users).

- If you need quick help to look up the list of shortcuts, press ▉, which shows a help overlay.

- If you don't like the mappings used, you can override these by turning on **Custom keyboard shortcuts** in the Labs menu. This causes the Keyboard Shortcuts tab to appear, and from here you can choose your own shortcuts, or add additional ones (so that one function may have two separate shortcut keys).

Themes tab

Most of the screenshots in this chapter shows the plain, vanilla Gmail theme, but it's possible to 're-skin' and personalize the general appearance using a range of themes provided:

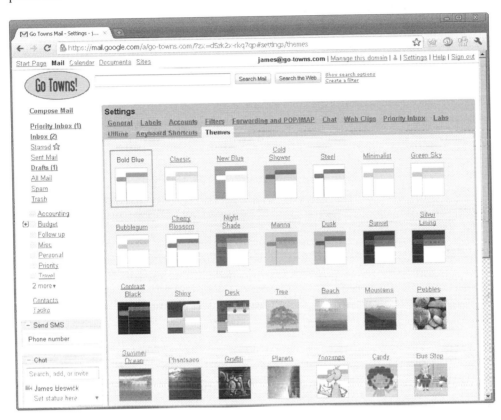

There are currently over 30 available themes, together with the option to set your own custom colors. To use a theme, simply click its icon and the application will immediately update its appearance. If you change your mind, click the **Classic** icon to revert back to the default look.

The themes option is a customization layer that can improve readability and usability for some users, but is primarily meant as a fun add-on. Themes don't affect any of the functionality, and only apply to the desktop version rather than the Android or smartphone clients.

Note that the logo displayed in the upper left of Google Apps (such as our sample 'Go Towns!' organization for this book) is set by the administrator in **Domain Settings ▶ Appearance** from the Google Apps dashboard (see Chapter 3), and is not affected by the user's theme.

Search: the real power behind Gmail

Generally speaking, Google's approach to user interface design is centered on simplicity. What could be simpler than the iconic landing page for **http://www.google.com**?

Of course, Google became famous through search and Gmail's search capability is second-to-none. Consequently, there are multiple ways to perform highly precise rapid searches across gigabytes of messages. In Google Search, the power behind that single search box is quite extraordinary: literally billions of web pages are explored in a fraction of a second.

The same algorithm has been used to make searching your mailbox just as fast, and there are three ways to do this. Getting comfortable with Gmail search will boost your productivity with the application, help you discover new uses for emails (such as task lists and notes), and make the transition from nested folders to labels more obvious. Additionally, since Gmail focuses on archiving rather than deleting, search becomes particular important given the sheer quantity of data that's being collected.

Using Keywords in the Search Box

Entering keywords is the way that 99% of searches happen, but it works a little differently to the way you might expect. Searching for a single keyword will return every message containing that keyword, but more complex searches are also available.

Entering one word will return all messages containing that word in date order:

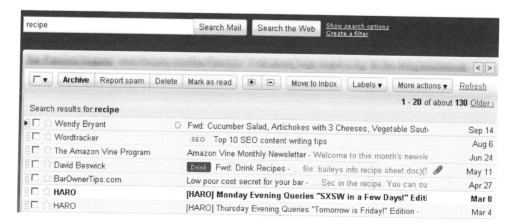

Entering multiple words will return messages containing *any* of the words. **American Airlines** may not just return a list of your flight bookings with that airline – it will return any email with the words American or Airlines.

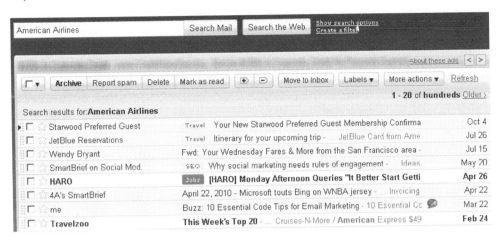

Entering words in quotes returns messages that match the words *exactly* as they appear (although capitalization isn't considered):

Using Search Options

Click the hyperlink next to the **Search** button to reveal a list of extended options to narrow down messages specifically:

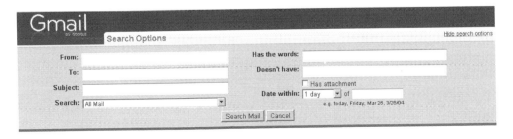

This is the most intuitive way to find messages where several pieces of information are known - simply enter the relevant fields and Google does the rest. But you might notice in the header of the search results that Gmail converts the fields to its search language, which brings us to the issue of advanced search operators.

Using Advanced Search Operators

You can enter complex search terms directly into the search box. The syntax takes a little learning, but once you become accustomed to it, you won't find any other system comes close in terms of speed and power.

A complete list of the most common operators is available at **http://mail.google.com/support/bin/answer.py?hl=en&answer=7190**, and these can result in search phrases that look at little complicated at first.

For example:

- **from:david has:attachment before:2011/01/01**
  Returns all messages from people called David that have attachments, sent before 1 January 2011.

- **label:work filename:pdf from:donald OR from:mickey**
  Returns all messages labeled 'work' with PDF attachments from people called either Donald or Mickey.

- **from:joanne (dinner OR movie)**
  Returns messages from anyone called that contain either the word "dinner" or the word "movie". If OR was excluded, the messages would have to contain both keywords in the braces.

- **after:2010/01/16 before:2011/02/1**
  Shows messages sent or received between January 16, 2010 and February 1, 2011. It's not necessary to include both before and after.

Don't worry if this looks strange - after a little practice, it makes more sense. Additionally, all of these search operators can be used when setting up filters.

Saving a Search with Quick Links

Although this is currently a Labs feature, it's likely become a standard option soon. Once you have created an advanced search, like any of those in the previous section, clicking **Add Quick Link** in the Quick Links gadget stores that particular view. For users who like the Explorer-style layout of Outlook, it can be replicated in Gmail by using this feature.

The Power of Contacts

Under the filters on the left-hand side of Gmail there's a link to Contacts, which is the virtual address book behind the messages. The information for people listed here is available in other Google Apps products, and also shared with other users in the domain.

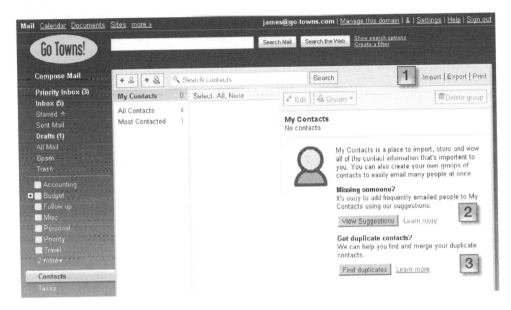

The Contacts view has three key general functions you're most likely to use initially:

1. **Import/Export**: Gmail can import contact information from a range of other email clients, which is critical if you need a migration plan. It can also export list of contacts already available if you've either enabled shared contacts or you need to extract a list of contacts after using Google Apps for a while.

2. **Suggestions**: although every person who sends you an email is added to contacts automatically, click the command button here to see a list of frequently contacted individuals who haven't yet been added.

3. **Duplicates**: although problematic for a single-user, it's almost endemic in organizations to find multiple duplicates of contact data. This feature helps to reconcile this information and provide one updated version for each duplicate.

> Currently, the Google Apps contact interface is different to the stand-alone Gmail version: presumably, these will become more similar at some point in the future.

Viewing and editing contacts

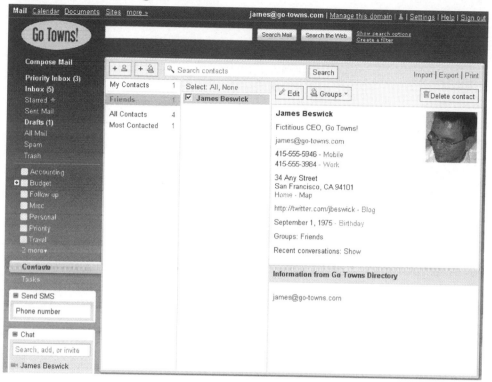

The contact view is broken into three columns:

- **Group**: this comprises the system-default groups (such as 'All Contacts') and any custom groups you create. Clicking on one of these filters the next column.

- **Contacts**: the names of all the people in the currently selected group.

- **Contact detail**: the specific information for the contact selected in column 2.

Use the **Groups** drop-down to add or remove the contact to the list of groups shown in the first column.

When you click the **Edit** button, text controls appear allowing you to make changes to any existing information. Many fields also have an 'add' hyperlink, which enables multiple entries - this means that emails, phones and addresses can be broken into various types such as home and work.

> After making changes to a contact, click Save and the updates will be immediately available to everyone in the domain if you have enabled contact sharing as the administrator.

Importing contacts

You can also import contact lists from many email programs - Hotmail, Outlook, Yahoo! Mail, Thunderbird - to name just a few. This works by first exporting the contacts from the source program in its default CSV or vCard format, and then clicking **Choose file** in Gmail to find and import the data. There are a few caveats:

- The Gmail importer doesn't understand groups so you will have recreate any groups once the import is finished.

- You can only import 3,000 contacts at a time (break your CSV file into smaller chunks if you exceed this limit).

- Any problematic contacts or errors are reported at the end of the process. Any conflicts will overwrite the existing data in Google Apps.

- The maximum size for a contact field is 32KB and anything longer will be truncated in the resulting contact record.

Sending email to groups

The Contacts tab is where you can add people to one or more groups, a frequently asked question from Gmail users. Once a group is created and it has members, you can send email to the group by just typing its name – as you enter text into the To, BCC or CC fields, it will be matched (just press **Tab** to auto-complete the whole name):

These groups are also shared across products in Google Apps, so inviting the entire Accounting Department group to an event is simple, or sending a view-only copy of a legal contract to your New Customers group takes just a moment. Similarly, if you have the Gmail application installed on your smartphone, all of these contacts and groups will be automatically synchronized with the device.

Sort by Sender

A common question from Outlook users is how to sort messages by sender – this can be done from contacts by selecting the person (or several people) and hitting the **Show** hyperlink next to 'Recent Conversations'. Unlike Outlook, if your contacts have multiple email addresses, it will show all the related messages grouped as one person (rather than one email address).

Top tips for Gmail

1. **Periods**: Gmail ignores periods in your email address (e.g. johndoe@gmail. com is the same as john.doe@gmail.com or j.ohn.do.e@gmail.com). This is helpful if you subscribe to third party newsletters – by placing the period some-where unusual, you can set a filter to identify those messages). It's also good for business cards since john.doe@yourdomain.com is more readable than the unpunctuated version.

2. **Labels**: you can include a label in your address so incoming mail gets labeled automatically. Mail sent to johndoe+work@gmail.com would automatically have the label *work* attached, yet reach the account just the same.

3. **Security**: for security reasons, you can't send executable files (such as those ending in dll, exe, and so forth). It's against the Terms of Service, and if there is a virus or other unexpected payload, the recipient could hold you liable.

4. **Tagging**: you can assign more than one label to a message, since labels are not folders (email clients using folders allow only one folder category per message). You can use this to avoid having multiple similar labels by combining keywords.

5. **Updates**: conversations are automatically updated so you will see a recipient's response if it arrives before you send your reply. An update alert appears in the bottom right of the screen, which helps avoid out-of-sync responses.

6. **Shift-click**: to select a range of conversations, instead of click each line individually, simple check the first, hold down **Shift** and then click the last. All the messages in between will be checked automatically.

7. **Google Talk** is small desktop tool that can provide an alert in the system tray when new messages arrive. This is helpful for monitoring new messages when your browser is closed. It also enables instant messages, phone and video chat outside the Gmail window.

8. **Previews**: in addition to the preview mode for graphical attachments, you can open PowerPoint presentations as a slideshow directly from Gmail (even on computers without PowerPoint) and Word/Excel files can be opened directly into Google Docs.

9. **Archiving**: the Archive button simply moves a message out of your inbox – nothing more, nothing less. This is the reason you can't archive sent messages, because they are never stored in your inbox.

Gmail Privacy and Advertising

Google's privacy practices are occasionally in the media, and Gmail hasn't avoided the questions of how the search engine giant treats your messages. There have been a number of frankly alarmist articles about Google spying on its users, so I think it's only reasonable to put this into perspective and discuss how the company is actually using your mailbox.

In a nutshell, Google is not reading your messages nor is it sharing them with anyone else. However, there are automated processes that do read your mail in order to eliminate spam, detect viruses, filter messages according to rules you create, and provide some of the intelligent features that help do useful things, like add meetings to calendars. These are no more insidious or intelligent than antivirus software on your PC, which also scans all your private data.

In order to provide a free service, Gmail displays ads on a sidebar, and this is also a source of consternation. Unlike other mail providers which provide ads regardless of message content, Google scans for keywords and displays targeted ads. This works in much the same way as the 'Sponsored Links' sidebar in Google Search – those ads are selected for relevance in the hope that you will find them useful (and therefore click one).

If your last five messages relate to booking a flight to Italy, you will likely see ads for flights, travel or attractions in Italy. The algorithm is smart enough to ensure ads are family-safe and sensitive – for example, if you announce a funeral, you won't see any ads. Ads are never attached to emails and do not bind with your message data in any way.

You can read more details about Gmail and privacy at
http://mail.google.com/mail/help/about_privacy.html.

Frequently Asked Questions

How do I ignore a conversation?

We've all been included on long email conversations that simply won't go away. Normally, it takes some manual deletion, since other email systems don't connect the conversation, and you rely on the same subject lines to kill the chatter. With Gmail this is a snap.

- From the **More Actions** drop-down, click **Mute**.

- Alternatively, use the keyboard shortcut 'M' (if you have shortcuts enabled).

If you accidentally mute a conversation, either click **Undo** in the alert immediately after or select **Move to Inbox** when reading the message. To find muted messages, simply search with the term 'is:muted'.

How do I schedule email in Gmail?

You've written your killer sales copy and want the email to go out later, or you're working late and want your boss to think it's 3am. Either way, you need to schedule an email to be sent at some point other than now. Unfortunately, there's no direct way to do this currently but there are some workarounds.

- You can save a message as a draft - click the **Save** button rather than **Send**. Then just wait until the scheduled time, find the message in the Drafts folder and click **Send**. This, of course, is the manual method.

- Since you can view your Gmail messages in Outlook, you can alternatively use Outlook's scheduling feature.

- If you don't have Outlook, you can use the free email client Thunderbird which has an extension called 'Send Later' which handles the task.

- If you need to send a simple email, entering the item as a description on a Google Calendar entry may just do the trick. Make sure that email reminders are turned on, the time period is set, and it will be sent at the appropriate time. It's limited solution - it does not handle complex emails, and the email clearly comes from the Calendar application.

How do I retract an email I didn't mean to send?

This is a perennial question about email systems which usually arises when an email goes out by accident. Unfortunately, there's no way to 'retract' a sent email in any system (Outlook's implementation of this only sends a second email to everyone requesting a retraction, but the original is still readable). Due to the fact there are many email clients and systems, once it's gone it's gone. But Gmail does have a couple of tools that attempt to make these accidents less likely:

- The **Undo Send** Labs feature adds a delay before the message is really sent, during which time you can cancel the action.

<table>
<tr><td></td><td>**Undo Send**
by Yuzo F</td><td>○ **Enable**
◉ **Disable**</td></tr>
<tr><td></td><td>Oops, hit "Send" too soon? Stop messages from being sent for a few seconds after hitting the send button.</td><td>Send feedback</td></tr>
</table>

- The **Don't forget Bob** Labs feature attempts to identify any recipients that may be missing based upon your previous email history:

<table>
<tr><td></td><td>**Don't forget Bob**
by Ari L, Naty L & Ron M</td><td>○ **Enable**
◉ **Disable**</td></tr>
<tr><td></td><td>Once you pick some email recipients, Gmail suggests more people you might want to include based on the groups of people you email most often</td><td>Send feedback</td></tr>
</table>

How do I attach multiple files to an email simultaneously?

You attach files by clicking **Attach File** but it's not immediately clear how to select multiple files at the same time. This is an easy one, and there's also a workaround:

- When the File Selector dialog appears, hold down the **Control** key to select multiple items. If you have a large list, click the first item, hold down the **Shift** key, and then click the last - you'll see all the items in between highlighted. Click **OK** to attach the selected files.

- The workaround is to add all the files to a ZIP file and attach the single resulting file. You will need to use either Windows' built-in compression feature or an application such as WinZip or 7Zip. The main benefit is that the email may be smaller, depending upon the type of files you're zipping up, and it may be easier for the recipient to download one large file, depending on their email client.

How can I view multiple messages at the same time?

Because Gmail is loaded in a browser window, it seems as though you can only see one thing at a time. When you compose a message, you cannot see your inbox, and when you reply, you cannot look up other messages.

This is true in the single window view, but you can easily pull your current task into a new window by client the **New Window** icon or hyperlink that appears in the top right.

How I can sort messages by sender, date, size - just as in Outlook?

All of these sorts can be performed using search operators - see earlier in this chapter for more details.

How can I make sure my email is secure?

There are several steps to this process, no matter what email system you use, and there's one Gmail-specific tip.

- Pick a strong password - see "Selecting a Password" in chapter 2. This is your first line of defense in almost any computer system.

- Make sure your computer is running the latest operating system patches, and the latest browser versions. Security problems are fixed by developers all the time, and keeping up to date here will keep most of the malware out.

- Turn on HTTPS - for personal Gmail, this is an option until the General tab of Settings. For Google Apps, it must be set by the administrator under 'Domain Settings'. HTTPS is slower than non-secure traffic (due to the overhead of making it secure) but is not noticeable in most situation. Turning this on stops others from listening to your email on open wi-fi connections at coffee shops, for example.

How do know when beta features are available?

System-wide notifications are usually shown in the top right of the window, next to your account name. Clicking the link will shown additional information about new features and announcements.

5. Google Calendar

Once you have created a Google Apps account, you can access Google Calendar by opening a browser and visiting either:

- **http://calendar.yourdomain.com**: if you set a custom URL for the service (see chapter 2), you can access the site on your own sub-domain.

- **http://calendar.google.com/a/yourdomain.com**: this is the default URL, which will always work even if you've set up a shortcut sub-domain.

In either case, you need to substitute *yourdomain.com* for the actual domain you registered or purchased in chapter 2. The first method is recommended purely because it's easier to remember, but they both lead you to the same place. You can also click the shortcut in the header of any other Google Apps page.

Note that the first time you sign into Google Calendar, you will need to set your default time zone. If you make a mistake or need to change your time zone in the future, access this from **Settings** ▶ **Calendar settings** ▶ **General**.

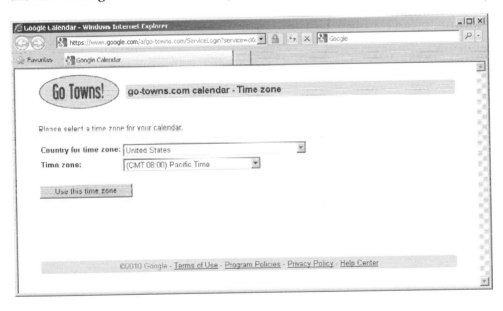

If you've become excited about Gmail and its possibilities for your organization, wait until you see Google Calendar. This may well be the simplest and most powerful time management tool ever created. The first time you open Calendar, there will be a brand-new empty calendar waiting for you, like the one on the next page.

The Basics

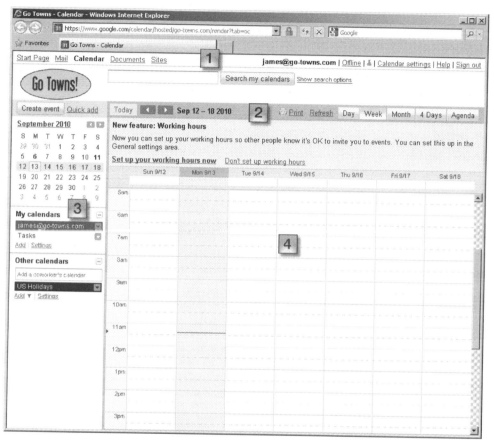

There are four main areas of the screen:

1. **Header**: the Google applications in your account are shown in the top left, while settings and help and shown on the right. A search box enables you to search all your events or the web.

2. **View**: switch between Day, Week, Month or Custom date ranges from the right, and navigate 'before' and 'after' using the arrows on the left.

3. **Calendars**: a list of the calendars you own or have access to, together with other publicly available calendars.

4. **Detailed view**: depending on the time frame selected from the tabs above, this shows the detailed event information for that range.

Creating an event

There are several ways to create events, but the simplest is to click the **Create event** command button in the top left, which gives you the most flexibility for building events.

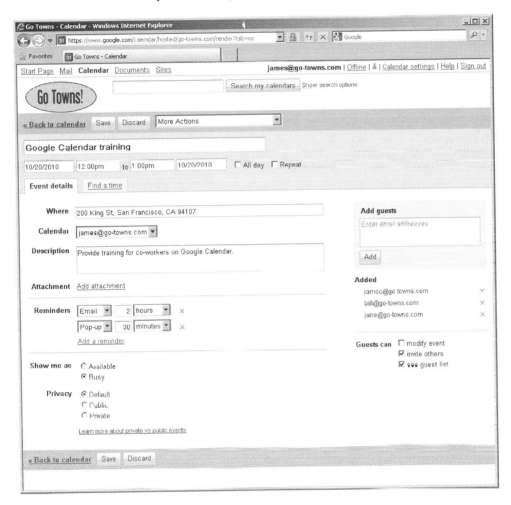

Most fields are optional, and the calendar entry can include the following:

- **What and when**: add the description, date, start time and end time. You can set an event as 'All day' by checking the box. We'll cover recurring events in a moment.

- **Where**: this can be informal (e.g. John's office) or an address. If Google can understand the address, it will map the location on some devices, and provide a clickable location link in Google Maps.

- **Calendar**: it defaults to your primary calendar but you can add the event to any calendar you have access to. You can only add an event to one calendar.

- **Attachment**: add a file from Google Docs, or upload another file type for sharing. You must ensure the guests have permission to see the attachment first, or will be invisible in their calendar.

- **Reminders**: you can set up to 5 types of reminder – emails and pop-ups will fire off at a scheduled time before each event (be aware that Pop-ups only appear if you are logged into Calendar).

- **Privacy**: here you can determine who can see the event details. 'Default' inherits the calendar's privacy settings. 'Private' means you and anyone else with 'Make changes to events' privileges (or higher) have access. 'Public' reveals all details to those with free/busy access, but doesn't make the event publicly searchable.

- **Add guests**: if you wish to include people not already included on the calendar you are modifying, add them here. You can also add any email groups you have set up, making it easier to schedule events for large numbers of people.

- **Guests can**: you can specify if invited guests can modify the event or invite others not currently included. Additionally you can choose to show or hide the rest of the guest list.

If you need to create a recurring event, click the **Repeat...** checkbox to show the additional event options:

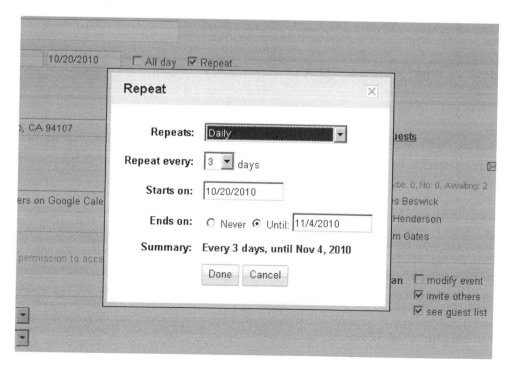

Set the interval in the first drop-down, and then the frequency of the interval in the second. The remaining options will change depending upon the interval type selected, and it's possible to create some fairly complicated rules (e.g. every 3 weeks, but only on Tuesdays and Fridays). Once you have set the start date and optional end date, click **Done** to schedule the event.

Even once a recurring event is scheduled, it's easy to make modifications to just one of the occurrences by clicking it in the calendar. When editing or deleting a repeating event, a confirmation box gives you the option to modify a single instance, every event in the series, or all future events.

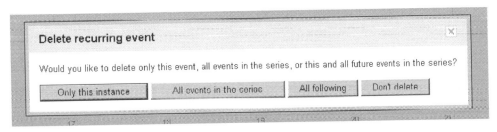

The second tab, **Find a time**, stacks the calendars of all attendees together to help find empty time slots common to everyone. Event guests can be set as required or optional to help make it easier to discover viable time slots. This feature is particular useful for scheduling resources such as meeting rooms.

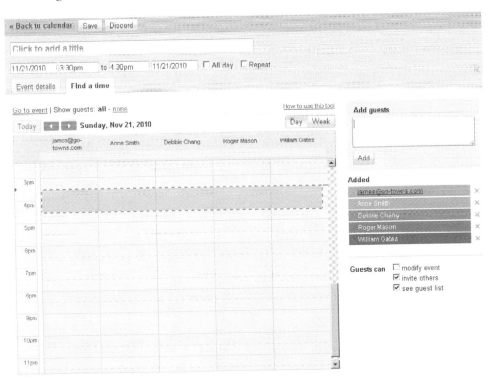

Reviewing events

Once you have a few events in the calendar, the day-planner view starts to fill up with solid boxes, showing the description of each event positioned at the appropriate time on the display. The screen will vary depending on whether the day, week, month or agenda view is selected (this is how the 'Week' view appears):

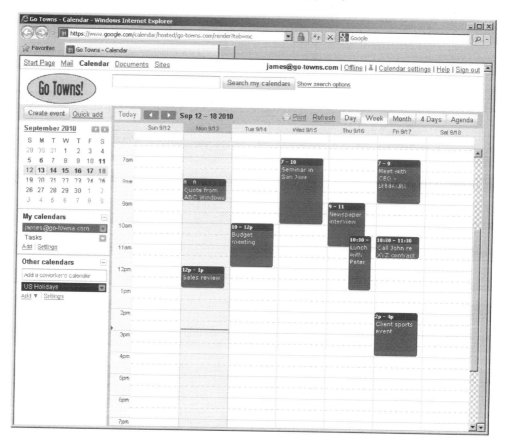

To view the event in detail (or make changes), click the appropriate box you want to edit and a screen similar to the Create Event screen will appear with the relevant fields pre-populated.

In this view, the options panel has moved off to the right and there are two new items:

- **Discuss this event**: other people with access to an event (and those in your Google Apps domain) can add comments.

- **Attendance**: as guests accept invitations, Calendar displays their responses. The email link can be used to send bulk emails to guests.

Once you have made changes as needed, click the **Save** button to update.

Calendar Settings

Click **Settings ► Calendar Settings** in the top right-hand corner of the screen to access your overall Google Calendar configuration. The default configuration will be fine for most users, but it's useful to know what can be changed.

The General Tab

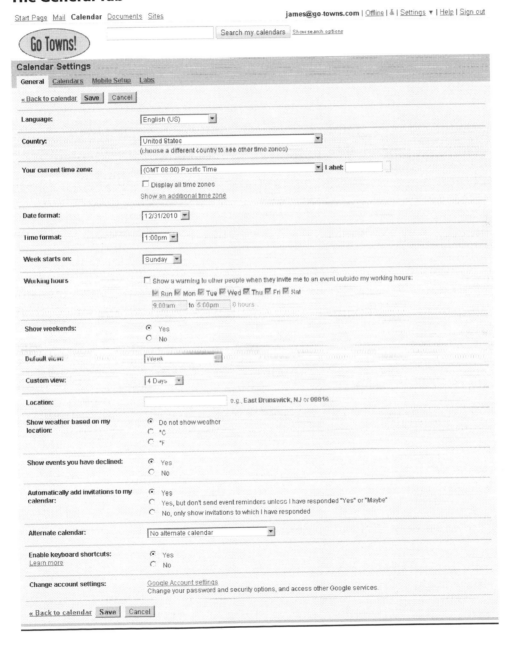

- **Language**: select your preferred language - this defaults to English (US).

- **Country**: defaults to the country you selected when you first opened Calendar.

- **Time zone**: defaults to the time zone you selected upon sign-up. A change in time zone automatically updates all events (e.g. meetings set at 5PM Central will become 7PM PST). You can also choose to show additional time zones.

- **Date/time format**: sets your date and time display preferences.

- **Week starts on**: sets the first day of the calendar week (only Sunday, Monday or Saturday are available).

- **Working hours**: allows you to specify your working days and hours, so that invitations set for times outside these will receive an appropriate warning.

- **Show weekends**: disabling weekends creates more space for weekdays in the events view.

- **Default view/custom view**: the view that appears when you first sign in to Calendar, and the time period for the custom setting.

- **Location**: some calendars use your location to determine content, such as the optional 10-day weather forecast.

- **Show weather based on my location**: adds a weather icon for the next 10 days in your calendar, using either Celsius or Fahrenheit.

- **Show events you have declined/automatically add invitations**: choose to show declined invitations in the display, and decide if Calendar should auto-accept incoming invitations to events.

- **Alternate calendar**: Hijri and Chinese calendar setting configuration.

- **Keyboard shortcuts**: these can be enabled or disabled here. A complete list of Calendar keyboard shortcuts is available at **http://www.google.com/support/calendar/bin/answer.py?answer=37034&hl=en**.

As always, once you have made changes, you must hit **Save** to apply.

The Calendars Tab

When clicking a calendar, you will be taken to the calendar details screen, described later in this chapter. If you delete a calendar, a prompt will appear to confirm if you simply want to remove the calendar from your profile or delete all the content in the calendar. Be careful with deletions since they are permanent.

The Mobile Setup Tab

Before you can receive SMS messages, you have to confirm your cell phone number. Enter the country and phone number and click **Send Verification Code**. Usually within seconds you will receive a PIN code on your phone, which you will need to enter in the confirmation screen.

> Although it's free to send SMS from Google, be aware that your cell phone provider may charge for incoming messages – check your plan for details.

The Labs tab

Go Towns!

Search my calendars   Show search options

Calendar Settings

General   Calendars   Mobile Setup   **Labs**

Google Calendar Labs: Play with our latest ideas. ⚗

Google Calendar Labs is a testing ground for experimental features that aren't quite ready for primetime. They may **change**, **break** or **disappear** at any time.

Tip: Some of these features will appear in a new panel on your calendar. To save space you can hide them by clicking the small triangle next to the panel.

Give feedback and make suggestions about Calendar Labs

« Back to calendar   Save   Cancel

Gentle Reminders
By Sorin M - Aug 2010

○ Enable
● Disable

Do you like pop-up reminders but hate how they rudely interrupt whatever you're doing? This feature replaces Calendar's pop-ups: when you get a reminder, the title of the Google Calendar window or tab will happily blink in the background and you will hear a pleasant sound. Alternatively, you can choose to use desktop notifications in Chrome.

Automatically declining events
By Lucia F - Mar 2010

○ Enable
● Disable

Lets you block off times in your calendar when you are unavailable. Invitations sent for any events during this period will be automatically declined. After you enable this feature, you'll find a "Busy (decline invitations)" option in the "Show me as" field.

Event attachments
By Sundaresan V and Oana F - Mar 2010

● Enable
○ Disable

Attach a Google document, spreadsheet or presentation to your event, or upload a file from your computer. Important: guests do not automatically have permission to view Google Docs attachments. You must share each attached document. Learn more

---

Event flair
By Dave M - Mar 2010

○ Enable
● Disable

Bring life to your calendar and organize your events with icons for things like flights, vacations, parties and meals. Note: icons added to events you organized will be visible to all attendees. After you enable this feature, click on an event and look for the "Calendar flair" gadget to activate.

Smart Rescheduler
By Dave M - Mar 2010

○ Enable
● Disable

Helps you re-schedule an event by analyzing everybody's schedule, evaluating conflicts, obtaining conference rooms and proposing the best meeting times. It's like magic.

Who's my one-on-one with?
By Sumitro S - Oct 2009

○ Enable
● Disable

Having a hard time figuring out who scheduled that event called "Lunch" on your calendar? This feature displays the attendee's name right on the calendar if it's just you and one other person.

Year view
By Dave M - Sep 2009

○ Enable
● Disable

Planning ahead and want to see the whole year at once? Adds a "year view" button to calendar.

Add any gadget by URL
By John L - Aug 2009

○ Enable
● Disable

Displays a box in the panel next to your calendar that allows you to add any gadget by specifying the URL.

Labs is where Google releases experimental extensions from their engineers, and you have to option to test-drive various features. As before, there are no guarantees about these add-ons and they may break or disappear (though I've personally never had any issues with Labs options).

The current list of Labs options includes:

- **Gentle reminders**: provides a less intrusive reminder pop-up.

- **Automatically declining events**: set times in your calendar when you won't be available, and invitations sent for these periods will be declined.

- **Event attachments**: attach Google Docs or files to an event (note that you must share a Google Document before attaching it).

- **Event flair**: provides a range of icons to categorize events visually.

- **Smart Rescheduler**: helps to reschedule events by checking the availability of all attendees and presenting available times that work for everyone.

- **Who's my one on one with?** When there's only one other attendee to an event, their name appears next to the event name.

- **Year view**: when the day, week and month views are not enough, turn this on to see the entire year at a glance.

- **Add any gadget by URL**: plug any gadget into the panel to the right of the calendar, just by adding the URL.

- **Dim future repeating events**, this helps emphasize one off meetings over regularly scheduled events.

- **Background image**: customize your calendar view by adding a background.

- **Free or busy**: for friends that share their calendar with you, it shows who is free right now.

- **Jump to date**: provides quick navigation to dates far in the future or past, skipping the need to get there month at a time with the standard navigation.

- **Next meeting**: counts down the days, hours and minutes until your next event.

- **World clock**: show the time in other parts of the world and provides additional time zones when you click an event.

Labs features are added and removed constantly, so you may find additional options are available.

Individual calendar settings: Calendar Details

Access this screen by clicking a calendar name from Calendar Settings or clicking the drop-down next to the My Calendars panel and selecting Settings. These settings only apply to a single calendar.

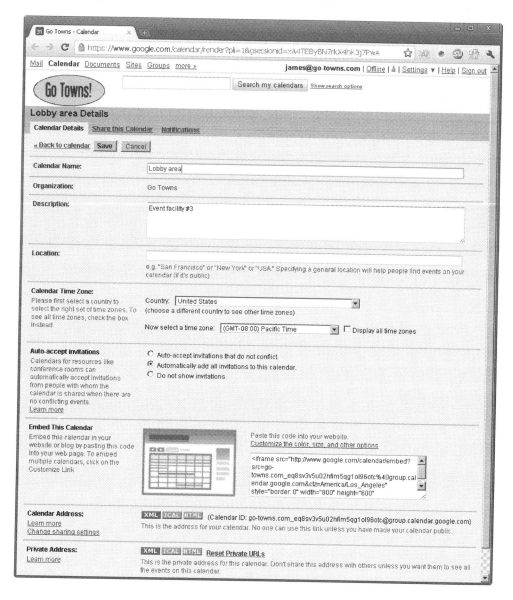

- **Basic**: the title and description helpful identify the calendar, while location can be used to provide map assistance if the calendar is public.

- **Calendar Time Zone**: is inherited from the general calendar settings, but can be changed on a per-calendar basis.

- **Auto-accept invitations:** inherited from general settings, but you may have calendars where the default needs to be different.

- **Embed This Calendar**: the calendar can be embedded as a gadget in web pages or Google Sites. We will cover this in detail later, but for now this is where you get the HTML code that makes it happen.

- **Calendar Address:** the public address for your calendar, allowing others to subscribe to your public calendar, view your events via feed readers, and view a read-only version directly in their browser. Your calendar must be public in order for this to work. To edit the amount of information available, click the **Change sharing settings** link.

- **Private Address:** designed for your use only. All of your calendar information is available via your private links, so don't share this address unless you intentionally want to the calendar public. If it advertently gets discovered, click **Reset Private URL** to get a new address.

Share This Calendar Tab

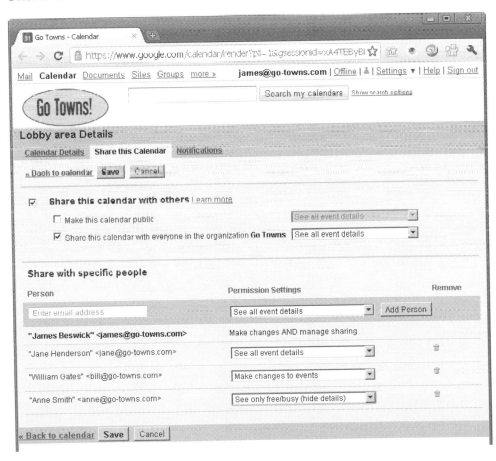

Checking **Make this calendar public** opens its contents to the world. You have the option of only revealing free/busy information too – for example, if you want clients to know when meeting times are available, but not see the details of meetings that are book, then check this option. Public calendars are Google-searchable, so use cautiously and don't use these to store personal information.

If you are using Calendar as part of Google Apps, you will see an additional option, enabling a calendar to be shared with users of your domain. To share with an individual, enter their email address and select their permission level. As users are added, they will appear in the list, and can be removed by clicking the trash can icon. For individuals, there are four levels of permissioning, from "Make changes and manage sharing" (effectively an administrative role) down to only showing free and busy information.

The Notifications Tab

Notifications settings on a calendar level apply to all events in that calendar, but are overridden by notification rules set on individual events.

- **Event reminders**: you can set up to 5 reminder types, each with a different time period. These are sent by email, browser popup or SMS message. Click **remove** to delete a reminder type.

- **General notifications**: you can receive updates for calendar-level events (eg. new and modified entries), or receive a daily digest.

If you haven't yet set up your cell phone, click the link at the bottom to return to the **Mobile Setup** screen. As always, click **Save** to commit any changes.

Multiple calendars in real life

A single calendar is useful but multiple calendars allow you to separate different projects, people and agendas without cramming everything into one view. Many users have just one calendar, but you can more easily separate events into types of calendar.

For example, by categorizing events into their own calendar, you can create:

- **A travel calendar**, showing hotel bookings, flight information and car rentals all in one location.

- **A team calendar**, specifying deadlines and upcoming work for several people.

- **A project calendar** for each project you are working on.

The reason why separation makes so much sense is due to the collaborative nature of Google Calendar – you can share one topic without sharing absolutely everything. By using settings for each calendar, you can then set general privacy levels without having to modify them every time, as you would with a single calendar.

To see how this works, our fictitious company *Go Towns!* has the following calendars:

- **A Team calendar** for team meetings and events.

- **A Personal calendar** for personal appointments.

- **A separate calendar for each event facility**, so we don't accidentally over book rooms. These are publicly viewable.

- **US Holidays**, since we apply a surcharge for events on those days.

- **UK Holidays**, as we market to British clients.

This seemingly-complicated combination of calendars takes only minutes to set up, and results in the screenshot below.

Adding a new calendar

There are five ways to add a calendar:

- **My Calendars ▶ Add**: this creates a default, blank calendar.

- **Other Calendars ▶ Add ▶ Browse Interesting Calendars:** provides access to read-only pre-populated calendars, such as holidays, sports events or even phases of the moon.

- **Other Calendars ▶ Add ▶ Add a co-workers calendar:** links to calendars of other users in your domain (where the privacy is set appropriately).

- **Other Calendars ▶ Add ▶ Add by URL:** Calendar can also show any iCal-compatible feed, given the URL.

- **Other Calendars ▶ Add ▶ Import Calendar:** this is most useful if you are transitional from Microsoft Outlook or any other iCal-compatible application, where you can export an existing file directly into Google Calendar.

Advanced features

Alternative ways to add events

Of course, having a calendar isn't much use unless you can make appointments and there are many ways to do this. Let's look at a few.

1. Quick Add.

Above the mini-calendar in the main screen is the **Quick add** option - click this to show the text field below.

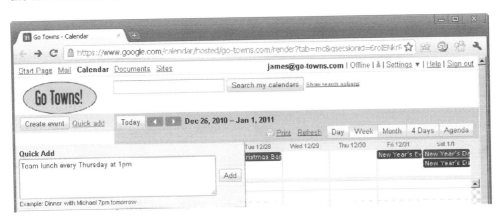

This simple feature is the fastest way to add natural language entries such as:

- Team meeting every Friday at noon.

- Charity tennis on Saturday at 2 with johndoe@yourdomain.com.

- Call New York at 3.

Calendar will interpret your event and place it on the chart. The trick to making this work well is to build your phrase using a 'what when who where' structure. Having said that, the algorithm has a good understanding of what you mean even breaking that rule, and can interpret words like 'every' to create recurring meetings.

2. Dragging directly on the calendar.

The most popular way to create a meeting - dragging on the calendar - has an immediate air of simplicity. Drag across the required time period, enter the event name and Google will drop the meeting straight into your default calendar. If you need to add more details, click edit event details instead. Calendar adjusts settings according to the current day/week/month view displayed.

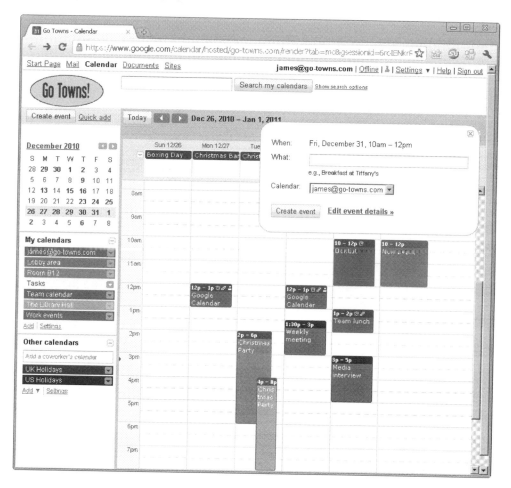

3. Adding directly from Gmail.

If Gmail detects an appointment within an email, you will see a box appear on the right-hand side offering to schedule the meeting directly in your calendar. This is especially useful for flight confirmations, restaurant bookings and so forth since the details are copied across with one click.

4. Creating appointments via SMS (text message).

Once your cell phone is verified with Google, you can create events by texting the details to GVENT (48368). This works the same way as Quick Add and is especially useful if your phone doesn't have full web access.

Embedding calendars

Back on the **Calendar Details** screen that I mentioned earlier (available under Calendar settings), there's a section that provides embedding assistance. A calendar doesn't have to exist only in the Google web browser view – it can be displayed as a gadget. A gadget is simply a box that drops onto a webpage, and contains content from another website or service. Gadgets are an intrinsic part of Google applications and help extend their functionality outside the Google environment.

This translates to the ability to display calendars in other locations – for example, you can place your company's event calendar on a website, without needing users to specifically visit Google Calendar. Later, we'll see how you can also place them in Google Sites.

When embedded into a webpage, the result looks like this:

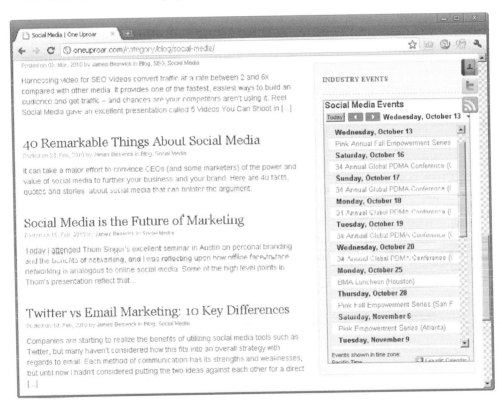

Everything outside the calendar is part of the company's webpage but the calendar itself is rendered as an embeddable gadget, seamlessly part of the display. The webpage includes a snippet of code to make this happen, which Google Calendar produces for you.

Click on the **Calendar Settings** link and near the bottom of the display you will see the **Embed This Calendar** section.

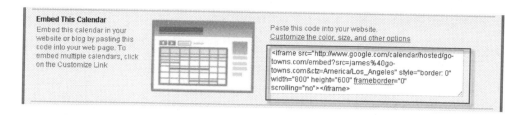

Embed This Calendar

Embed this calendar in your website or blog by pasting this code into your web page. To embed multiple calendars, click on the Customize Link

Paste this code into your website.
Customize the color, size, and other options

```
<iframe src="http://www.google.com/calendar/hosted/go-towns.com/embed?src=james%40go-towns.com&ctz=America/Los_Angeles" style="border: 0" width="800" height="600" frameborder="0" scrolling="no"></iframe>
```

The HTML in the box will render the calendar automatically, but usually you will want to customize the height, width and appearnce first by clicking the link called **Customize the color, size, and other options**.

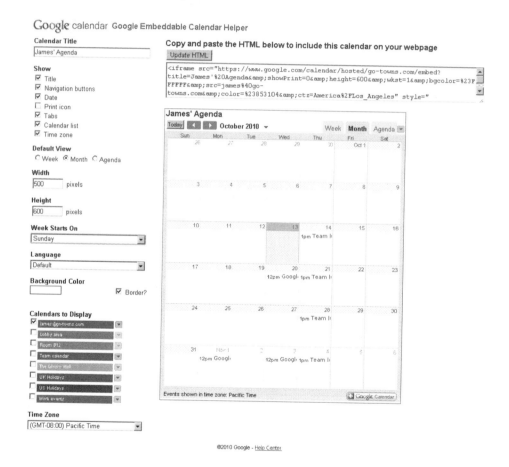

On the left hand side, you can select which features to display in the embedded gadget. As you change these, the preview on the right will change. Once you are satisfied with the layout, click **Update HTML** and the HTML will appear below.

You don't need to be web designer to use this – it's as simple as cut and paste. Just paste the HTML into the source of a webpage, and the gadget will make itself appear when the page is loaded into a browser.

Top tips for Google Calendar

1. Check if the weather in your area suits your events – go to **General ▶ Settings** and select Celsius or Fahrenheit under 'Show weather based on my location'. This will place weather icons directly on your calendar for the next few days.

2. Receive your schedule via text message by texting "day" to 48368 to receive today's agenda. Send "next" for tomorrow's agenda. Be aware that SMS charges may apply depending upon your cell phone plan, so check with your carrier.

3. Resource allocation is a snap – if you have conference rooms, vehicles or staff that can't be double-booked, simply create a calendar for each one and set 'Auto accept invitations that don't conflict' in settings, so that bookings administer themselves.

4. If you use a Blackberry, click the Sync link in the top right corner for information on how to synchronize with your device. Google Sync is a PDA client that downloads Google Calendar events onto your BlackBerry, and uploads Calendar events from your BlackBerry (two-way synchronization over the air).

5. If you really prefer to use Microsoft Outlook, there's a synchronization tool that will use the data from Google's Calendar servers but show the results in the Outlook application.

6. If you have an event that repeats on the same days each week, but it doesn't fit the Mon/Wed/Fri or Tues/Thurs combinations provided, no problem. Select 'Every week' and a series of check boxes appears for each day of the week that you can click to generate any customized weekly recurrence.

7. If you want to see your upcoming events in Gmail, there is a Calendar widget available in Labs. Once activated, this will add a panel that shows a list of upcoming events for all of your visible calendars.

6. Google Docs

Google Docs consists of documents, spreadsheets and presentations – the Office equivalent of Word, Excel and PowerPoint all in one browser. Google uses the term document to mean *file* – spreadsheets, word processing files, presentations and PDFs are all documents.

There have been a variety of free Office look-a-likes in the desktop environment, the most popular being Sun's OpenOffice project (**http://www.openoffice.org**). The web has also seen some impressive browser-based versions such as Zoho (**http://www. zoho.com**). But I would argue that Google Docs is more than just another Microsoft Office clone principally because of its revolutionary collaboration features and cloud storage capabilities.

Google Docs used to be an umbrella for the underlying Word, Excel and PowerPoint-type applications, acting little more than launch point or screen to list all your documents. Fairly recently the functionality has changed: it's become more like a cloud-based file server, allowing users to store any type of file, and not just the ones created by the underlying applications. The Google Docs screen is the equivalent of Windows Explorer, although we'll discuss some of the differences later, and provides a view of all the files you have stored in the Google Apps platform.

In this chapter I'd like to show you how I you can use Docs to move all your organization's files away from your PCs and file servers towards the Docs cloud where you have more granular permissioning and the ability to access them anywhere with an Internet connection. You benefit from the security of having files invisibly backed up multiple times by Google's infrastructure and the simplicity of working on documents with coworkers without emailing them back and forth.

Once you have created a Google Apps account, you can access Google Docs by opening a browser and visiting either:

- **http://docs.mydomain.com**: if you set a custom URL for the service (see chapter 2), you can access the site on your own sub-domain.

- **http://docs.google.com/a/mydomain.com**: this is the default URL that will always work even if you have set up a shortcut sub-domain.

Alternatively, if you are logged into another Google Apps service such as Gmail, you can reach Google Docs using the application links at the top of the page.

The Basics

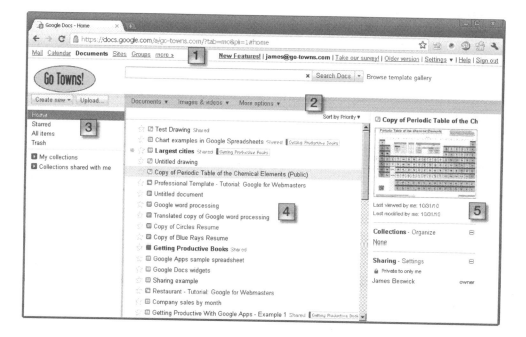

The main screen is comprised of 5 general areas:

1. **Header**: links to common Google services, search functions, settings, informational updates, help and sign out.

2. **Filters**: show only documents that meet basic criteria such as whether the type of file, who the document was created by, and who it is shared with.

3. **Collections**: documents can be grouped and organized in collections (which are like Windows folders), and any collections you have created appear here.

4. **Document list**: the list of documents that you either own or share, the main repository of your data, filtered by whatever criteria you have selected.

5. **Preview area**: shows a graphical preview of the currently selected item, together with information about how it's shared and organized.

This is the standard view of the Docs List, reminiscent of Windows Explorer but there are differences. Explorer organizes files based upon physical characteristics such as drive letter, folders and user-specific locations (e.g. "My Documents"). In the Google Apps view of the world, this is not useful, intuitive or desirable for several reasons, which are worth covering in more detail.

The differences between Google Docs and Windows Explorer

First, in Explorer it's easy to lose track of where documents live since your network connectivity can change – unplugging a USB drive or disconnecting from a shared drive will cut you off from the data in those locations. The drive-letter approach puts the organizational onus upon the user to know where their information is living, and different users often have different drive mappings.

If you've ever been confused about which VNC server you are viewing through Citrix and why your network directories are missing, you probably understand the pain here. In the traditional view, the technology behind where the data resides gets in the way of actually using it.

It's also easy to end up with multiple versions of the same document, all with slight variations made by different people, with some residing on C:\ drives and others stored in emails buried in Outlook. This can be really difficult to follow and invariably requires somebody to attempt to piece fragments of versions back together. While programs such as Microsoft Word have document revision capabilities, these are complicated for the novice user, and still rely upon a single physical file.

The familiar Explorer world can also lead to user-unfriendly errors when other people are editing files, such as the Windows classic, "The file *filename* cannot be opened or saved. It may be opened or locked by another application or you may not have access to it". When you receive errors like this, you can spend more time tracking down who has the file open than actually doing the work on the file.

In the spirit of collaboration, version control and the power of search, Docs List shows all your documents you've ever touched (or been granted access to) in the Docs List. This resolves the above problems:

- Documents all live here, with no exceptions. If you have Internet access, you have access to all your data.

- Docs tracks all versions of a file forever – no need for cryptic names like "Marketing Plan_Final_FINAL_10-NOV-10.DOC". This is automatic and invisible.

- Docs openly invites people to share in real time without conflicts, and those users have real names like "Jane Smith" rather than PC-type names such as user "smithj029 on XPPC2992".

    Because all changes are tracked forever, it's worth educating your users not to type frivolous or offensive messages since these become a permanent record of the file.

131

Organizing & Finding Documents

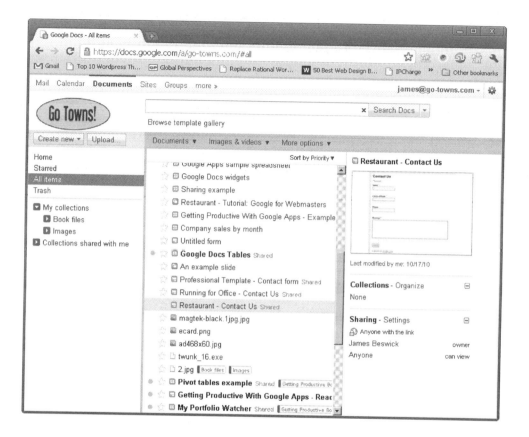

As you create or upload files to Google Docs, they will appear in the list of files on the main screen without any pre-defined organization. Since the number of items can grow to be overwhelming, there are a variety of organizational tools available to help group items, flag important documents and change the way the documents are listed.

There are several ways to organize and filter your documents in Google Docs. The most general appears on the top-left, where there's a choice of:

- **Home**: shows all documents, with the exception of those where "Don't show in home" has been selected.

- **Starred**: shows all documents where a star has been added.

- **All items**: lists every document available to you, regardless of if it has been put in a collection or starred.

- **Trash**: when you delete a file, it is moved to the Trash collection. Items in trash are not finally deleted until you select this filter and click **Empty Trash**.

Beyond these basic filters, more granular options are available in the header above the file list:

- **Documents**: this drop-down allows you to filter documents by type (e.g. by spreadsheet, presentation, PDF, etc.)

- **Images & videos**: here you can choose to view only graphical files, and the list will change to a thumbnail preview mode.

- **More options**: this drop-down shows more complex filters, based around visibility and ownership. For example, you can select files only visible to you, or only those shared with other users; or show files that you created compared with those shared with you. We will cover sharing in more detail later on.

- **Sort by**: finally, you can determine the list order, sorting by priority, title, when a file was last modified or last opened. 'Priority' is determined based upon a number of signals designed to identify the files that are most important to you.

These filters only allow you to change the list of documents based upon some attribute of the individual files. If you want to search across the contents of a given document, the omnipresent search bar at the top of the screen will help.

> The search bar is the same fast, powerful search as the one used in Google's web-based search. You can scour gigabytes of Google Docs files in a split-second with this function.

The search bar will show instant results as you start typing in the drop-down shown below. Clicking any of these will open the document directly or alternatively press **Enter** to update the document list to show the results.

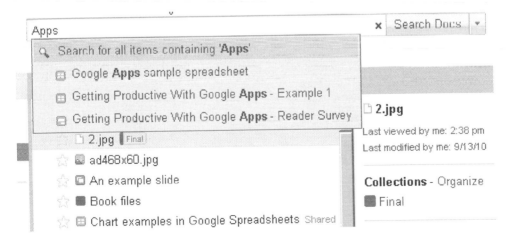

133

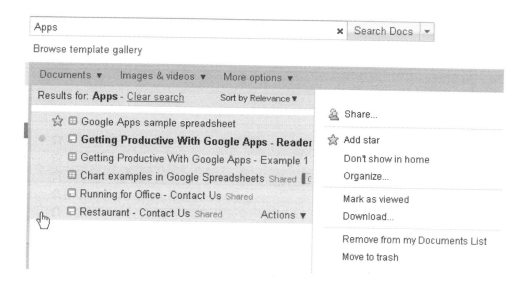

With the search results displayed, it's possible to select one or multiple files to perform additional actions. Clicking a result anywhere other than the title will select a single file. Holding down **Shift** or **Ctrl** allows multiple files to be selected (the behavior is the same as Windows Explorer). With several files selected, use the menu in right-hand pane to share, organize or download the files.

Using collections to group documents

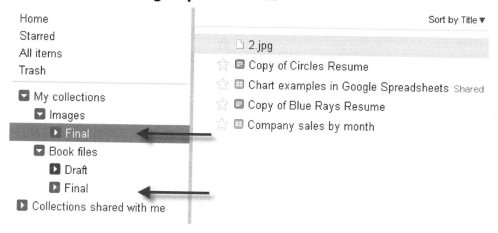

Collections are the Google Docs equivalent of a folder in Windows with a couple of major differences:

- With Windows folders, a file can only exist in one folder. With Google Docs, a document can belong to more than one collection. In some respects, this makes collections similar to labels in Gmail.

- With Windows folders, a folder can exist inside another folder, but not inside two folders in different places in the hierarchy. With Google Docs, collections can be nested inside other collections, and can even exist in two different places.

This is powerful but also a little confusing for new users. While collections appear as a hierarchy, the same document may appear in more than one collection, and even a collection may be displayed in more than one place in the hierarchy. In the screenshot above, the Final collection is a member of both the Images and Book files collections. Although it appears twice, there's actually only one collection, and any documents placed in the Final collection will show in both locations.

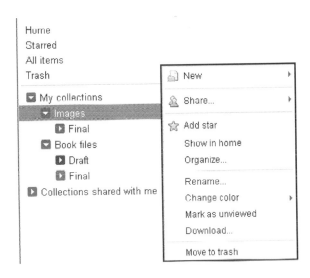

Right-clicking any collection shows a list of actions that can be performed on the collection. The key options are:

- **New drop-down**: select the type of document you wish to create, and it will be automatically added to the collection.

- **New ▶ From template**: build a document based upon an existing template from the user-developed library available, directly in the selected collection.

- **Share**: displays the 'Sharing settings' dialog box, allowing you to share entire collections in one step.

- **Organize**: this produces a dialog showing the collection hierarchy, where you can then change where a collection belongs.

- **Change color**: the collection arrow's color can be set manually here.

- **Download**: you can download the contents of an entire collection here.

Sharing Documents & Collections

Sharing is the simpler approach to access rights used in Google Docs and, unlike many other systems, users are empowered to choose who can see their data without needing to have I.T. specialists configuring permissions.

In the desktop world, if you want to share a document, you have to save the file, attach it to an email and find some innovative way of appending any updates to the original document. And if you want to share with the world, this involves putting the document on a web server somewhere, a task most users wouldn't undertake lightly. In Google Docs, you're just a few clicks away from setting up your sharing rules.

The default level of sharing

Before we get started, Google Apps allows administrators to set the default visibility for all newly-created files. In Chapter 3, you configured this default visibility for documents (under **Service Settings ▶ Docs** in the Google Apps control panel) - depending upon your selection, new documents will be:

- **Private**: only the document's creator can access it, unless others are invited.

- **People in the domain who have the link**: the file is invisible to others in the domain unless you provide the link.

- **Everyone in the domain**: new documents are visible to everyone.

The control panel also allows you to select whether files can be shared with users outside your domain.

Sharing options

You can share one document, several documents or entire collections:

- **To share a single file**, ensure the document is selected in the main window, and look for the sharing panel in the lower right. This shows who has access to the document already, and you can make changes by clicking **Settings** (see screenshot below).

- **To share multiple files**, hold down **Shift** or **Ctrl** to select the documents and then click **Share...** in the right-hand panel.

- **To share a collection** click its drop-down arrow, and then click **Share... ▶ Sharing Settings**.

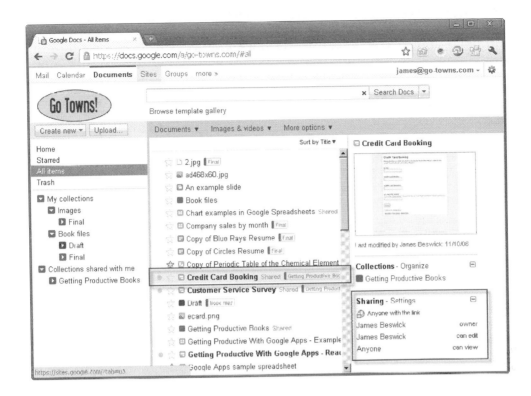

Whichever method you choose will lead to the **Sharing settings** screen:

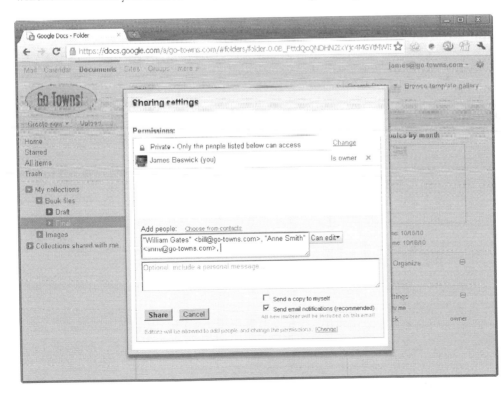

This screen shows the current level of access in the first line (Private, in the example above), together with the list of users who currently have access. You can remove a user's access by clicking the ☒ icon to the far right of their name.

To add additional users, enter their names just under the 'Add people' label (click Choose from contacts if you need to look up their information). There are two types of access level available:

- **Can edit**: the user can read and make changes to the document.

- **Can view**: the user can read the file but is prevented from making changes.

After you have added the users' names, you also have the option to send a notification email and include an optional personal message. If your colleagues are used to sharing documents with you, skip sending the invitation by unchecking the 'Send email notifications' option. Otherwise, hit the **Share** button to deliver a notification via email.

Sharing visibility

In the example above, the file has the most narrow level of visibility - Private - which means that only the document's creator and individuals named explicitly can view or change its contents. In total there are five types of document sharing available, in addition to some publishing options we'll cover later. This gives you broad flexibility for providing document-level permissions - click **Change** on the first line to see what's available:

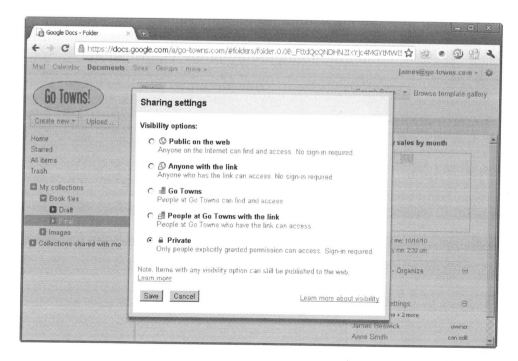

The five visibility levels, starting with the least restrictive, are:

- **Public on the web**: this is the least conservative option, making your spreadsheet available to the whole world and searchable by search engines. People can access the document anonymously with no Google account required. Clicking **Public on the web** will create a world-wide URL that provides access, and follows the format **http://docs.google.com/Doc?docid=?uniquekey**.

- **Anyone with the link**: users need to know the link to reach the document, which they also do anonymously, but the file is not indexed by search engines.

- **Your organization (e.g. Go Towns)**: the document is visible to everyone with a Google Apps account in your organization. They must be logged in to view.

- **People at your organization with the link**: just like the second option above, but the document is not visible to external users or those not logged in with a ID from your Apps account.

- **Private**: this is the default option, so only the creator and those specifically given access can gain access. If you don't grant access to anyone else, it remains completely private to you and invisible to everyone else.

Although you are most likely to use the Private option and invite individuals when sharing is needed, there may be times when it's useful to share documents with people you don't know. For example:

- Publishing online forms for customers or vendors (select Anyone with the link).

- Displaying your user or sales numbers on the web (select Public on the web).

- Sharing the underlying data for an academic paper (select Public on the web).

Note that when you choose any of the first four options, a checkbox will appear that allows to you to grant editing rights (by default the first four are read-only).

Be careful with these options, since it's possible to publish a document globally that can be edited by anyone *anonymously*. I'm not convinced there's ever a need to allow this, as it exposes your document to general vandalism on the Internet, but it's easily possible in these settings.

> If this concerns you as an administrator, you have the option to disable external sharing on your domain from the Google Apps control panel - see Chapter 3 for details.

Sharing options at the document level

If you open any Google document by clicking its title from the Docs list, there are some additional sharing options at the document level that are not available from the Docs List window.

Click the **Share** drop-down to view:

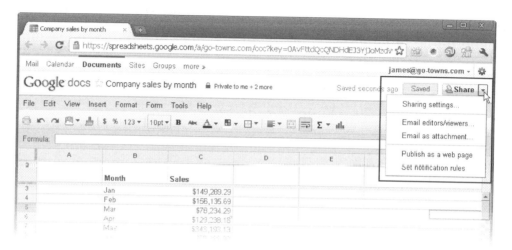

From this menu you can:

- **Email editors/viewers**: send a message to everyone with access to the file. This provides a simple way to email everyone associated with a document without going to Gmail and manually entering the recipient list.

- **Email as attachment**: Google Docs will convert the document to its equivalent Microsoft or OpenOffice format (or PDF if required), and send it as an attachment. This feature is useful if you are working with people without access to Google Docs or your domain, or users who prefer to use the desktop applications.

- **Publish to the web**: this generates a URL for an HTML version of the document. You can choose here if the document should be automatically republished as changes are made, and if the whole spreadsheet should be published or just a single worksheet.

- **Set notification rules**: you can opt to receive notification emails if changes are made to either the document or the list of collaborators. Select from the type of changes you are interested in, and then choose if you want real-time emails or daily summaries.

Creating and Uploading Documents

Creating a new document

Click the **Create new** drop-down and select the document type you want to create and the corresponding application will open in new browser tab or window. In the next few chapters we will be reviewing each type of document in detail.

Editing an existing document

In the Docs List, click any file to open – Google Apps launches the corresponding application automatically and displays its contents. Any changes you make to the document are saved every few seconds, so if you lose your Internet connection or your computer crashes, not much data (if any) will be lost. The **Save** button in each application is mainly for peace of mind but it's largely redundant in Google Docs.

Uploading documents

In addition to the files you create within the various Google Apps applications, you can also use the storage space as a cloud-based file server. This means that any graphics, videos or other document-types used in your organization can be moved from your file server into the Google Apps file space.

The major benefits here are that Apps tracks version changes, makes automatic back-ups, and allows you to access the files from anywhere with an Internet connection. You can also shares these files with the same granular permissions as any Google Doc.

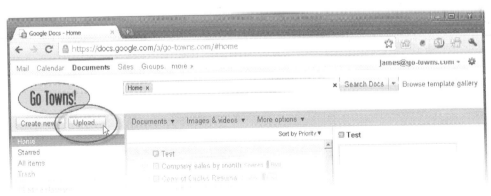

You can upload any file type to Docs (including compressed zip files and executables) by clicking **Upload...** above the folder list. From the upload dialog (see screenshot below), you can either drag and drop files directly to the files panel, or click **Select more files** - either way, you will see the list of filenames waiting to be uploaded.

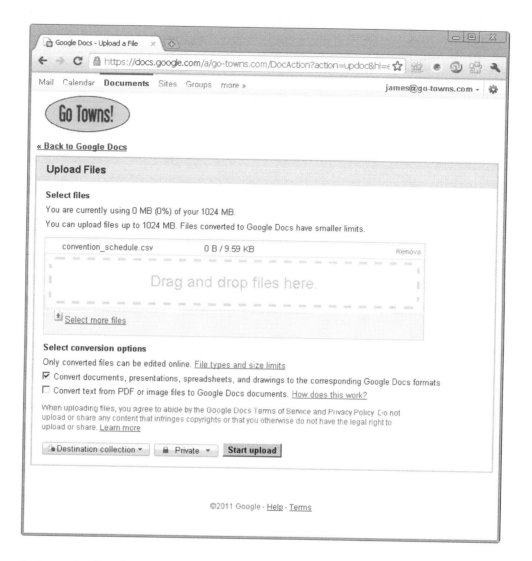

Before uploading there are four additional options:

- **Convert files to Google Docs formats**: Docs with convert the original Word, Excel or PowerPoint documents to their Docs equivalents and allow editing online.

- **Convert PDFs or image** to text using optical character recognition (OCR) to render editable text from non-editable files.

- **Destination collection**: by default, uploaded files are not grouped into a collection unless you specify a target collection here.

- **Sharing**: choose between the five visibility levels covered earlier.

Once you have selected the files and checked the desired options, click **Start Upload**.

Converting files to Google Docs format

If you convert upload files to their equivalent Google Docs formats, one benefit is that the resulting documents do not count towards your storage quota. However, there are size and format limits in conversion:

- **Documents**: doc, docx, odt, sxw, rtf, txt and html formats, up to 1MB per file.

- **Spreadsheets**: xls, xlsx, ods, csv formats, up to 1MB per file.

- **Presentations**: ppt and pps formats, up to 10MB per file.

- **Drawings**: wmf format only, up to 2MB per file.

One caveat about file conversion is worth remembering: Google Docs is not Microsoft Office. This means the conversion process yields an approximation of its content rather than a faithful duplicate, and your uploaded version may have significant differences compared with the original. – this is especially true for complex files utilizing the advanced features available in Office.

> **Do not upload all your files and delete the originals without checking that the converted version is satisfactory**

Take a look at the example on the next page, which shows a Word document with styles, clip art and a table. Once this docx file is converted by Google Apps, many differences are apparent, including missing style attributes, different fonts and table formatting. The same is true for Excel spreadsheets: charts, pivot tables, complex functions and other advanced features are ignored in the upload, although formulas are preserved.

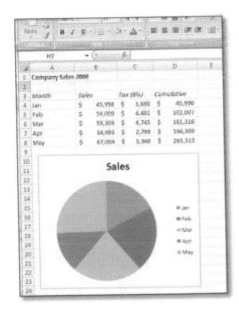
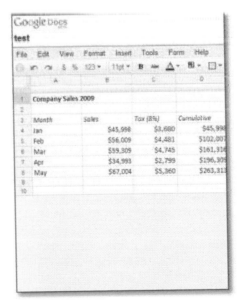

The Original Microsoft Word Document:

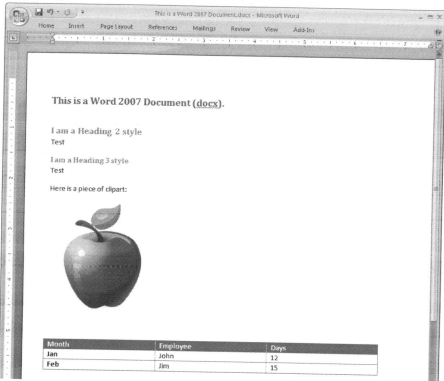

The Google Docs Version:

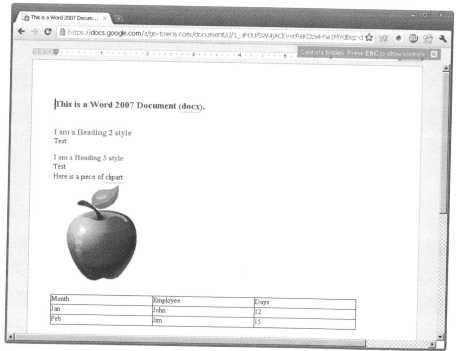

Using templates

You may have used templates in desktop office software but the Google library is more dynamic and user-driven. Click **New ▶ From template...** to show the list of templates available:

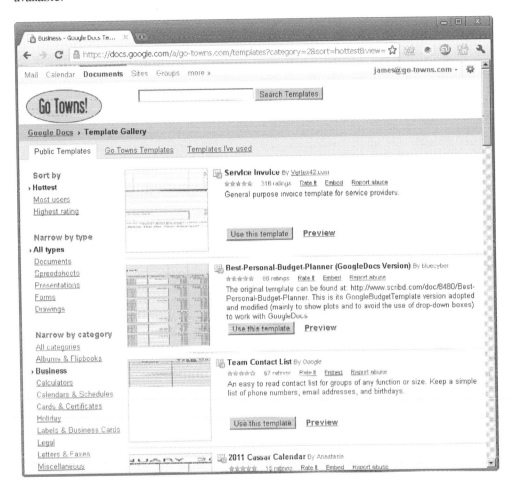

The tabs across the top filter the templates based upon type:

- **Public Templates**: the entire universe of templates.

- **Templates I've used**: only templates you have used before.

- **Organization Templates**: ones that have been designed by your domain's users and shared internally (this feature is only available on the Premier version).

On the left, you can apply additional filters by document type, popularity, category and language.

For example, search for 'Cityscape business cards' and click **Preview** to see what the template looks like. After, click **Use this template** to create a copy as a new document. As you make changes, these do not affect the underlying template, but become part of a new document that remains private to your profile (unless you choose to share the document).

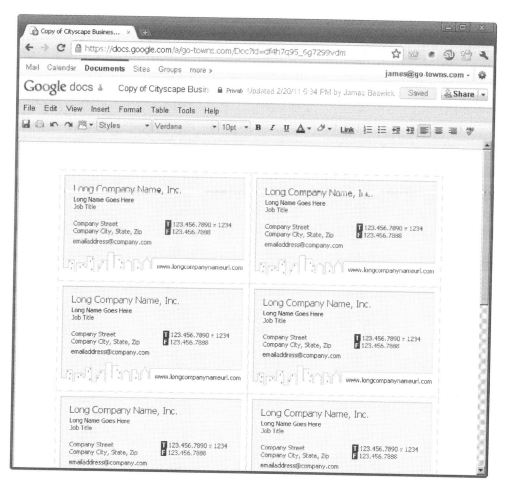

Templates are a great way to share common organizational documents such as invoices, quotes, letters, faxes and so on. To submit your own templates:

- Click **Submit a template** from the main templates page.

- Click **Choose from your Google Docs** and locate the document you want to submit to the template directory.

- Provide a description and up to two categories for your file, and finally click **Submit Template**.

Google Docs Settings

Click the **Settings** icon in the top right to access the general settings for Google Docs:

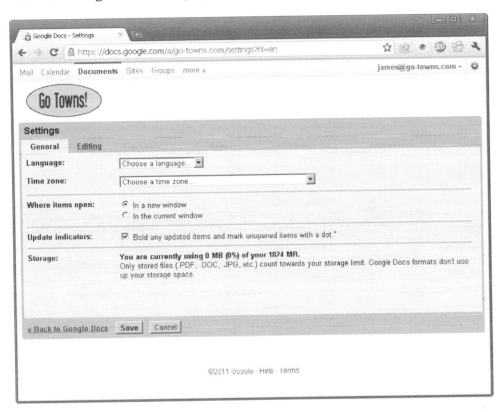

There are fewer settings than in Gmail or Calendar. In the **General** tab you will see.

- **Language**: determines the language used for Google buttons, labels and displays, rather than the document language.

- **Your current time zone** is adopted from when you created your Google Account – change it here if necessary.

- **Where items open**: choose to have documents open a new tab or window (default) or the same browser window.

- **Update indicators**: this shows recently updated or new items in bold.

- **Storage**: a measure of how much of your storage quote is currently used. Native or converted Google Docs files don't count towards your quota - only third-party non-Google documents are included.

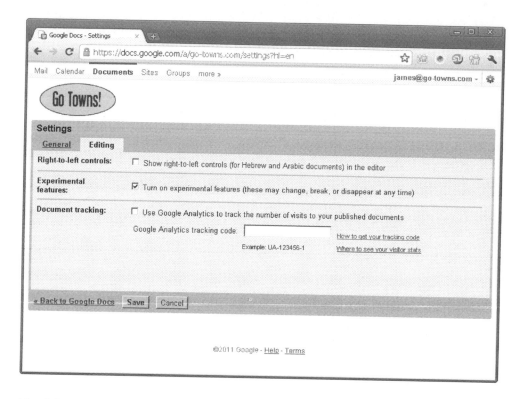

The following options appear on the Editing tab:

- **Right-to-left controls** alters the default (left-to-right) layout for Western languages to the Hebrew and Arabic default.

- **New version of Google documents**: choose to use the latest or the legacy version of the document editor.

- **Document tracking**: if you use Google Analytics, enter your tracking code here, and visitor statistics will populate in your Analytics dashboard.

Frequently Asked Questions

When I put shared files in a folder, why don't the other users see the folder?

Google Docs does not share how you organize data simply because users may disagree on how it is organized. If you put the Marketing Budget spreadsheet in a Marketing folder, the accounting department may choose to file it in a Budget folder. The correct folder depends on your point of view, so Google allows individual users to label shared data independently of each other.

When a document exists in two collection, are there two copies?

No. Although collections look like Windows folders or directories, they're more like tags or the labels used in Gmail. A document assigned to two collections really has two tags, so it appears twice in the collection hierarchy, but isn't copied anywhere.

How can I stop sharing a document with a colleague?

Select the document by placing a checkbox next to it and then click Share. In the resulting dialog box, click the 'X' icon next to any names you want to remove from the shared list, or click 'remove all' to make the file visible to only yourself. Unfortunately, this can only be done one document at a time – although you can share multiple documents in one action, removing permissions doesn't work the same way.

Can I collaborate with colleagues who don't use Gmail?

Yes. Enter their email addresses in the share dialog, and they will receive an email alert. They will need to create a Google Account to access the document, but they do not need Gmail.

Where is my data really being stored?

Google stores your files securely in multiple locations within their infrastructure, so in the event of any failure in their data centers, your data is still accessible. In terms of which drive or folder location, these concepts don't exist in Google Apps – all your data is just 'stored' in the Docs List.

Why can't a share a folder with 'Anyone with the link'?

Google temporarily disabled this feature at the time of publication.

I don't understand the sharing visibility options. What's the safest?

For most organizations, 'Private' will be the safest and most commonly used, since it ensures any new or uploaded documents can *only* be seen by their owner. For these files to be shared with anyone else, either inside the domain or externally, the owner must explicitly configure this.

Can I synchronize my Google Docs list with Windows Explorer?

Yes - there is a desktop client called Gladinet (**http://www.gladinet.com**) that can map to your cloud storage space to a drive letter in Windows Explorer. This allows you to open and save documents in desktop applications directly to your Google Apps storage area.

7. Google Word Processing

The word processing part of Google Docs is somewhere between a web development tool like Expression Web and a blogging platform like WordPress. Although it has some of the capabilities of a desktop word processor such as Microsoft Word, it lacks many of the more complicated formatting features and advanced functions.

This is largely because it is a browser-based web-page editor, and every document you produce can be exported to HTML and CSS. On the one hand, this doesn't perform much like Word, so getting documents to print perfectly can be awkward, but on the other, the ability to produce browser-friendly documents has its own advantages, especially if you tend to share online rather than print.

The collaboration element is also a major selling point — just as with Spreadsheets, other users can make real-time edits, so building and refining content is easy. Up to 50 people can edit the document and collaborate simultaneously (the document becomes view-only if more people join). This makes it ideal for editing text-heavy work in a team environment.

The usefulness of this feature depends on what you are doing. If you're in a team of lawyers working on changes for a lengthy legal contract, Google Docs will provide an infinitely better platform for sharing and editing the document simultaneously. But if you are working solo trying to design marketing materials with intensive graphics, text effects and precision placement, then you won't gain much from using it, and would probably be better off using a desktop alternative.

As with other parts of Google Docs, it's worth trying out the application to see if it suits your needs. It handles resumes, letters, contracts, essays, assignments and most documents with a simplicity that's hard to beat, just as long as being restricted to standard fonts and vanilla layouts isn't too important. Don't forget you can also upload documents from desktop word processors, as discussed in chapter 6, and collaborate on these as an alternative to emailing the file around, which is especially useful if some users do not have the desktop application installed.

To get started, go to **http://docs.google.com/a/yourdomain.com** (or http://docs.yourdomain.com if you have configured shortcuts in chapter 2) in your browser, replacing yourdomain.com with your actual domain. Alternatively, click the **Documents** heading from any Google service. Within seconds, the application will load in your browser window.

The Basics

From the main Google Docs window, click **New ▶ Document** to start the word processing application. The word processing interface is the simplest of any of the Google Apps products, with only three major areas:

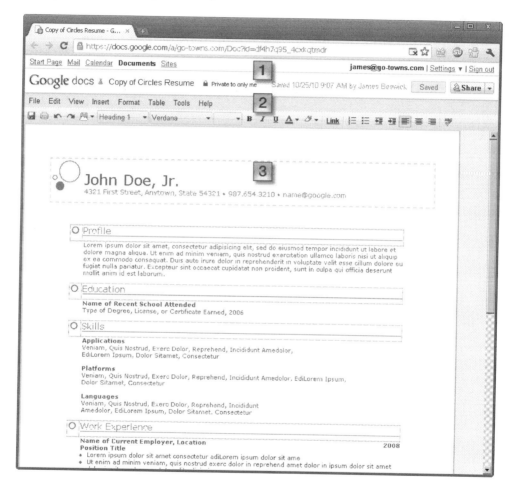

1. **Header**: links back to Google Docs, other services, account settings, sharing and saving options.

2. **Menus**: all of the application's available functions are grouped into menus and the main formatting toolbar.

3. **The document**: the content of the document itself uses most of the screen display.

Toolbar functions

Starting from left to right, here are the main controls, which will be familiar if you have used word processing applications before:

- **Save**: Google saves often, but if you want to force a save immediately, click here.

- **Print**: opens a printing viewing version of the document.

- **Undo/Redo**: backtrack on changes, and reapply if needed.

- **Web clipboard**: copies the current selection to a Google-hosted clipboard. Unlike the desktop clipboard, this allows multiple items to be stored simultaneously, and allows efficient pasting between different computers and applications. The web clipboard follows the logged-in user from browser to browser.

- **Styles drop-down**: apply heading and paragraph styles.

- **Fonts**: limited to a general range of browser-friendly fonts.

- **Font size**: changes the font size of the select range (currently only 8 to 36 point sizes are available).

- **Effects**: there are a range of character styles: bold, italic, underline, foreground and background colors.

- **Hyperlink**: attach a URL to text (so it appears <u>like this</u> and can be clicked to visit another webpage).

- **Insert Image**: allows you to upload an image from your local computer, enter an image URL, or search Google Images for content.

- **Numbering/bullets**: automatic numbering and indentation for lists.

- **Indentation controls**: change the position of the left indent of a paragraph.

- **Justification**: choose between left, center and right justification.

- **Spell check**: any spelling errors in the document are highlighted in yellow. Click again to hide these errors.

The File menu

- **File ▶ Upload**: links back to the main Google Docs Upload window, described in chapter 6.

- **File ▶ See revision history**: provides a history of every revision to the document. Click a revision to see the state of the document and optionally revert back to the selected version. Once you revert back, you will lose edits made since that revision.

- **File ▶ Rename...**: replace the default *Untitled* name of the document.

- **File ▶ Make a copy...**: creates a duplicate of the current open document.

- **File ▶ Download as**: a range of file types are provided, including OpenOffice, Word, PDF, RTF, text and HTML. This is an easy way to create PDFs for distribution, or use the document formatting for a webpage (HTML).

- **File ▶ Save**: saves the latest state of the document, but is largely redundant since Google Docs will automatically save the document every few seconds. This option is grayed out when there is no additional information to save.

- **File ▶ Print settings...**: set additional printing options here, namely page orientation and size, margins and annotations. The size is limited to A4, Legal and Letter sizes. If page numbers are enabled, you can set their position in the drop-down to the right.

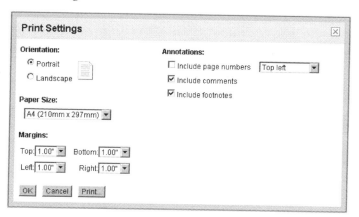

- **File ▶ Print preview...**: opens a printer-friendly preview of the document.

- **File ▶ Print as webpage...**: opens a new window with an HTML version of the document ready for printing.

- **File ▶ Print**: renders a printer-friendly version of the document ready for printing.

The Edit menu:

- **Edit ► Cut/Copy/Paste**: these are the standard commands using the operating system clipboard, which is different to the Web clipboard mentioned earlier.

- **Edit ► Find and Replace...**: shows options beneath the toolbar to help find and replace text strings in document. The drop-down shows advanced options such as using case-matching and regular expressions.

- **Edit ► Edit HTML and Edit CSS**: Google Docs produces standards compliant documents in HTML and CSS. For advanced users, it's possible to change the underlying code to add features not natively supported in the editor.

  Note that this feature only appears for older Google documents - for newer documents, click **File ► Download as ►HTML (zipped)** to see the underlying code.

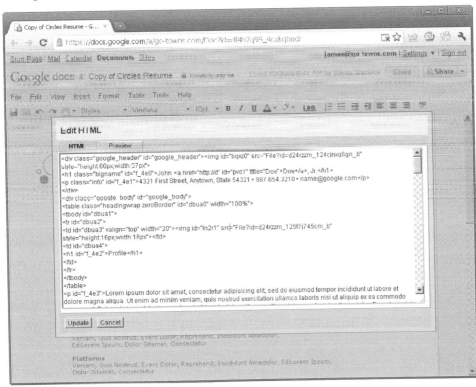

The View menu

- **Fixed-width page**: when unchecked, text is wrapped to approximately the width of the page size. When checked, it wraps to the width of the browser window.

- **Webpage preview**: shows the document as an HTML webpage.

- **Hide controls**: turns on a full-screen mode to maximize the screen space for your document. Press `Esc` to exit this mode.

- **Show footnotes**: toggles the display of footnotes.

The Insert menu

- **Image**: allows you to upload an image from your local computer or embed from a URL. Click **More image options** to set custom size, position and text wrapping. You can also create a link to the original image by checking the box (the equivalent of setting an `<a href...>` in HTML).

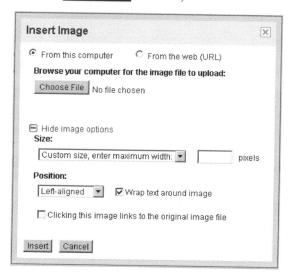

- **Drawing**: you can add a Google Drawing to your spreadsheet using this option. The Drawing part of Docs is covered in chapter 9, and can be used to add headlines and graphical elements with more flexibility than using cell-based text or inserting images.

- **Table**: opens the table dialog, covered later in this chapter.

- **Link**: attach a URL hyperlink to text (so it appears <u>like this</u> and can be clicked to visit another webpage).

- **Equation**: add a mathematical equation at the current cursor position.

- **Comment**: a comment is like a sticky-note appended to the text and appears in the right-hand margin.

- **Footnote**: allows you to add notes to a paragraph that will appear at the bottom of the page when printed or published. These appear in the left margin while editing.

Beswick, James (2011)

7. Google Word Processing[#]

The word processing part of Google Docs is somewhere between a webpage development tool like Expression Web and a blogging platform like WordPress. Although

- **Special characters**: for accented words such as café, or symbols such as © or ¼, these are located here, together with specialized characters for music, math, braille and arrow directions.

- **Horizontal line**: the equivalent of adding a `<hr/>` tag in HTML, this adds a horizontal break at the current insertion point.

- **Page break (for printing)**: use the page break to force where Google Docs should separate your document.

- **Header/Footer**: create or edit page headers and footers to your document, which will be added automatically to each printed or exported page.

- **Bookmark**: adds a hyperlink to a specific place in your document, which can aid navigation, particularly with long files and can be used to create an index or table of contents.

- **Table of Contents**: adds a basic table of contents based upon the usage of bookmarks and headings 1, 2 and 3 in your document.

The Format menu

- **Document styles**: sets the default font and font size, line-spacing and background color for the document (with the option to save these settings for all new documents).

- **Align**: choose between left, right, center and justified for the current selection (also available on the toolbar).

- **Paragraph styles**: applies a preset style (also available from the toolbar).

- **Clear formatting**: strips the current text selection of any styles, formatting or other HTML markup.

The Tools menu

- **Translate document**: creates a copy of the document translated into one of 53 supported languages using Google Translate. As with all automated language translations, you should check the output for accuracy.

- **Check spelling/clear spellcheck**: highlights any typographical errors in yellow (these can be cleared with 'clear spellcheck').

- **Select language (for spelling)**: your default dictionary is determined by your account's country setting but it can be overridden here.

- **Word count**: provides document statistics for both the current selection and the entire document, including various readability measures.

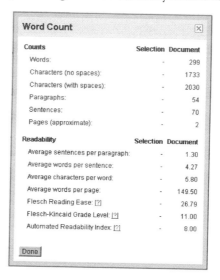

- **Manage document bookmarks**: shows a list of the document's bookmarks, any of which can be deleted here.

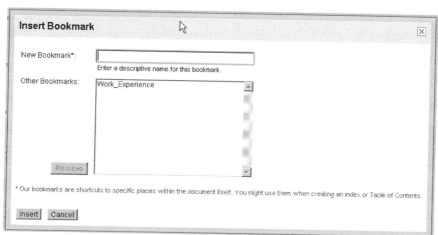

Word processing features

Paragraphs and headings

Pressing **Enter** creates a paragraph block, and each block can have its own style applied. Styles in Google Docs are more like headers in HTML, indicating which parts of the page are headings versus regular text. There are no formatting preferences associated with styles in Google Docs.

Comments

Comments can provide notes on content for editorial or review purposes, and appear on any printed or exported version of the document. The name of the editor and a timestamp is appended to the note. The icons in the corner of the comment enable you to reply to, delete or close it.

Inserting images

Click **Insert ▶ Image** to import a graphic into your document (or click the shortcut on the toolbar) and you will see this dialog:

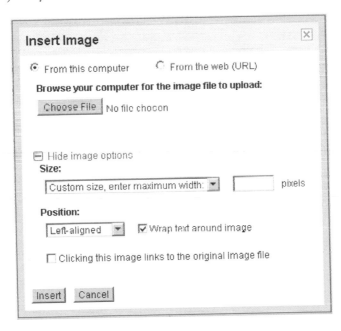

Click **Choose File** to locate the graphic file on your computer or network, or enter a URL to use an image on the Internet. Specify the size and text wrapping options before clicking **Insert**. Once the image appears in the document, you can then use the justification buttons on the toolbar to change its page position.

Table of contents

The table of contents provides a range of predefined numbering styles – once selected, the table is inserted at the current point in the document.

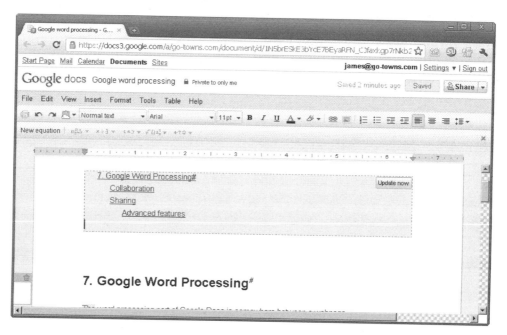

This tool extracts paragraphs that have heading 1, 2 and 3 styles applied, and indents the results. Unless you use these styles, the table of contents will be blank. As your document changes, you can update the table of contents by hovering over its contents and clicking the **Update** hyperlink.

> If you export the file as HTML, the table of contents becomes a collection of hyperlinks that help users navigate the page.

Footnotes

Footnotes differ from footers because they associate a section of reference text to specific content in the document and move dynamically so the reference text always appears on the same page (and with a footnote number). The footnote numbers are maintained by Google Docs, so adding new footnotes does not require you to change the numbering of previous footnotes.

As with comments, click **Insert ▶ Footnote** at the point in the text where the footnote reference should appear and type the footnote's comment. You can apply formatting attributes (bold, italic, etc.), and a footnote window appears next to each occurrence in the left margin. In the printed version of your document, these footnotes appear at the bottom of the page. If you export as HTML, any reference becomes a hyperlink.

Adding and modifying tables

Tables are a useful layout device for presenting certain types of data (especially information that usually resides in spreadsheets). Click **Table** ▶ **Insert table**:

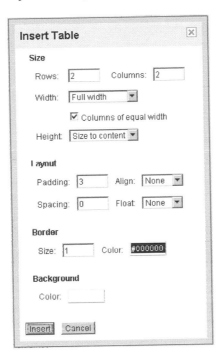

By default, a table will stretch to the width of the page with columns equally sized, and row heights automatically adjusted according to content. You can override these options in the width and height drop-downs. Click the Insert button to drop the new table into the document at the current cursor position.

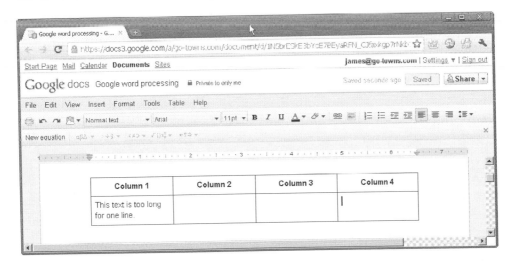

To modify the table, place the cursor somewhere within the table to activate the options in the Table menu. Most of the same options are available if you right-click within the table instead:

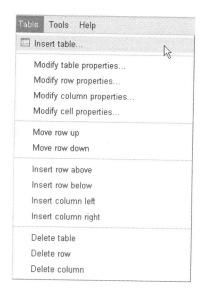

Tables in Google word processing no longer support some of the HTML styling that used to exist, allowing for so-called liquid layouts.

Tables can be nested within other tables by inserting the cursor in a cell and selecting **Table ▶ Insert table**. This works the opposite way if you're used to spreadsheets, where the same effect is created by merging adjacent cells – here the tables are distinct, and you can apply separate formatting rules to the nested table and parent table.

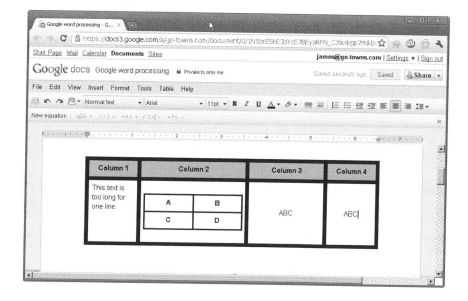

8. Google Spreadsheets

Spreadsheet applications have become one of the most important classes of business management and decision support software available. Microsoft Excel is the most famous of them all, but there are a variety of alternatives including OpenOffice Calc, WordPerfect Office Quattro Pro and Lotus SmartSuite 123.

Spreadsheets essentially automate calculations in tables of data, and provide all basic computations (addition, subtraction, etc.) together with proprietary formulas (such as calculating interest on a loan, or the number of days between two dates). The contents of a spreadsheet consist of rows and columns, and one spreadsheet document - called a workbook in Excel - may consist of multiple individual sheets.

One of the reasons that Microsoft Excel has become the predominant spreadsheet product is that it offers a broad range of different charts, features and functions, together with its own macro programming language. The Google Spreadsheets product is not a fully-fledged replacement for Excel, since it cannot substitute the more sophisticated features. Excel addicts who routinely use all the formulas and charting functions will probably find the Google offering somewhat lacking.

Having said this, Google Spreadsheets has its own list of features that it does very well. Simplicity is the major selling point, and although it only has a fraction of Excel's interface, that will suffice if you use Excel in a limited way - which most people do. Secondly, where Google really shines here is that there's no finer tool for collaboration. The reaction of first-time users when they start editing a shared spreadsheet is usually one of awe, since updates from other collaborators appear in real time seamlessly. Contrasted with Excel's idea of sharing, which is primitive to say the least, and it's easy to see why many users consider Google Spreadsheets an upgrade to Excel.

In the business environment, the decision to use Excel or Google Docs is not necessarily an "either/or" choice: many firms find they use a combination of both platforms, and there are major cost-savings if you can identify those users in your organization who don't need the Office installation and can use Docs instead. Since most spreadsheets created only use the most basic spreadsheet functions - sums, averages and conditional statements - all of these can be managed in Google Spreadsheets perfectly well.

To get started, log-in to Google Apps from the URL you configured in chapter 2, and click **Documents** from the list of the services at the top. From here select **Create new** ▶ **Spreadsheet** to open the spreadsheets application.

The Basics

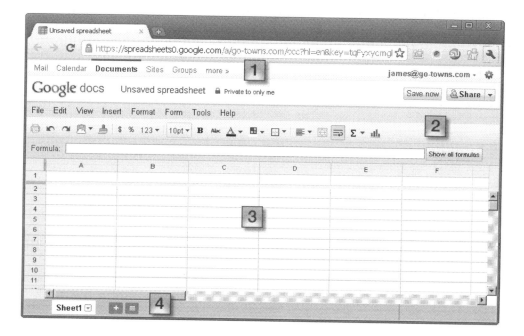

There are four main parts of the Google Spreadsheets interface:

1. **Header**: providing links to other Google Apps services, announcements and application settings. When new features are rolled out, you might also see a link to the previous version in case you want to opt out of beta participation. Saving and sharing options also appear in this area.

2. **Menus**: as with Excel, almost all spreadsheet functions are organized here with many repeated in the toolbar and right-click options available. Beneath the main menu you will see the application toolbar for common functions. This area also contains the formula bar, which shows the formula of the currently selected cell.

3. **The spreadsheet**: consisting of rows and columns, the cells of the spreadsheet are where you place calculations. You can also overlay images, charts and gadgets in this area. You can modify the size of rows and columns by dragging the separator line that appears between the row and column labels.

4. **Sheet tabs**: each sheet in a document is represented in this area and clicking between tabs moves the focus from one sheet to another. Any one spreadsheet file may consist of numerous child spreadsheets.

If you've used Microsoft Excel before, this layout will seem very familiar.

Toolbar functions

Excel has a large number of toolbars available (especially in the more complicated Ribbon control in Office 2007 and later). In Google Spreadsheets, there's only one application toolbar available. From left to right:

- **Print**: opens the printing dialog.

- **Undo/Redo**: backtrack on the latest sequence of changes or reapply if needed.

- **Web clipboard**: copies the current selection to a Google-hosted clipboard. Unlike the Windows clipboard, this allows multiple items to be stored simultaneously, and allows efficient pasting between different computers and applications. The web clipboard follows the logged-in user from browser to browser.

- **Paint format**: if you select a cell with formatting, click this function and then select another cell, the formatting will be copied from the first cell (the contents are not copied). This is similar to the Format Painter function in Excel.

- **Number styles**: click to apply default numerical styles to a range of cells (e.g. currency, percentage, or a drop-down of common defaults)

- **Font size**: changes the font size of the select range (currently only 6 to 36 point sizes are available).

- **Effects**: there are a range of character styles: bold, strike-through, foreground and background colors, and cell border style.

- **Justification and alignment**: choose between left, center and right justification, and top, middle and bottom cell alignment.

- **Merge**: you can merge the highlighted range of cells together into a single cell, which can be useful for adding titles or other text that would be broken by the column layout. Clicking again while a merged cell is selected will return the range to its original layout.

- **Word wrap**: check this option to enable or disable word wrap within a cell or range. When unwrapped, a cell's height will automatically adjust for its content.

- **Common formulas**: a list of the most common spreadsheet formulas, together with a link to the formula builder.

- **Insert chart**: opens the chart dialog box.

The File Menu:

File	Edit	View	Insert	Format	Form	Tools	Help

- **Import**: imports any supported local spreadsheet file to Google Docs, but rather than forcing the creation of a new document can be placed more precisely (e.g. it can be inserted into a new sheet, replace the existing sheet, etc.)

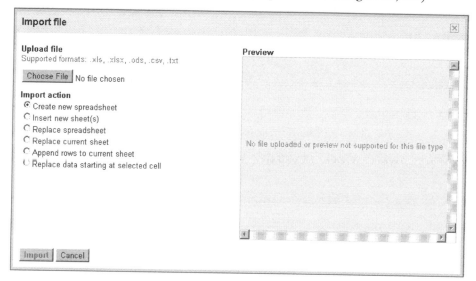

- **See revision history**: shows every revision made to the document. Click a revision to see the state of the document and optionally revert back to the selected version. Once you revert back, you will lose edits made since that revision.

- **Spreadsheet settings**: sets the country and time zone, which default to those in your account. These settings impact formatting rules and the time used in the revision history.

- **Rename...**: replace the default Untitled name of the document.

- **Make a copy**: creates a duplicate of the current open workbook.

- **Download as**: a range of file types are provided, including CSV, HTML, text, Excel, OpenOffice and PDF. This is an easy way to create PDFs for distribution, or use the document formatting to create a webpage (HTML).

- **Save**: saves the latest state of the worksheet, but is largely redundant still Google Docs will automatically save the document every few seconds.

- **Print**: this option doesn't invoke the operating system's standard print dialog - instead, it provides a series of options to lay out a PDF file.

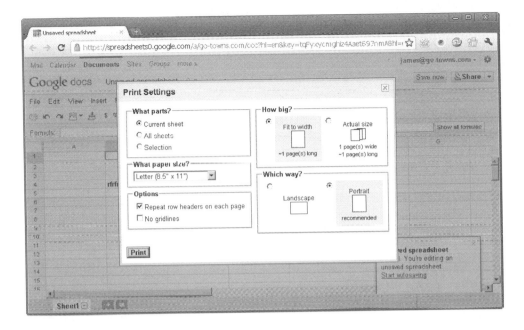

The basic printing options (shown above) include:

- **Print area**: choose between current sheet, all sheets in the file, or the highlighted selected. When you select all sheets, the output will automatically set each tab to a different page.

- **What paper size?** Select from common paper sizes (Letter, Legal or A4). There's currently no way to used customized paper sizes.

- **Options**: check the first box to force row headers across every page, and check the second to hide table gridlines.

- **How big?** This scaling option lets you optimize the layout to fit the width of the worksheet to the width of the paper - or just print at actual size. Under the icons, the dialog shows an approximation of how many sheets of paper will be used.

- **Which way?** Choose from landscape (sideways) or portrait (tall).

The print-friendly version will open in a new browser window ready for sending to the printer. Printing is one of the weaker parts of the Google Apps suite, since it is designed primarily as an online tool.

There is currently no elegant way to add header or footers, or have any granular control over the output. One workaround is to export the file to a desktop spreadsheet application.

167

The Edit menu:

- **Cut/Copy/Paste**: these are the standard commands using the operating system clipboard, which is different to the Web clipboard mentioned earlier.

- **Paste format only**: unlike regular paste, which will overwrite the contents of a cell with both the values and formats of the source, this option only copies the formatting.

- **Paste values only**: as above, but instead only pastes the values and ignores the source's formatting.

- **Named Ranges**: creates and manages named ranges for the active workbook (see later in this chapter for more details).

- **Find and Replace...**: shows a dialog to help find text strings in either the current sheet or all sheets in the current dialog, and optionally replace any matching text.

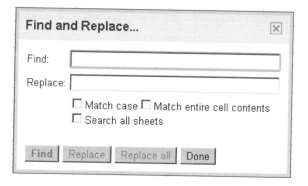

The View menu:

- **Normal view/List view**: toggles between the spreadsheet view and a more compact list view. List view is useful when sharing sheets to more than 50 users, accessing on a slow Internet connection or certain types of mobile phone.

- **Hide gridlines**: toggles the display of the lines between cells.

- **Show formula bar**: shows a row above the column heading displaying the formula in the active cell. When **Show all formulas** is checked, the cells display their underlying formulas rather than their results.

- **Compact controls**: hides the Docs Header above the spreadsheet.

- **Hide controls**: hides the Docs Header and menu bars above the spreadsheet (press Escape to return to Normal), which helps maximize the amount of screen space available for the spreadsheet.

The Insert menu:

- **Insert row/column**: this dynamic option also appears if you right-click column or row heading, allowing you to add one or more rows or columns. Depending upon the size of your selection, the option will update itself accordingly.

- **Comment**: a comment is like a sticky-note added to a cell, and can be used to provide additional information about its content. It doesn't affect the calculation of the cell's contents or formatting, although commented cells have a small orange marked in their upper right-hand side. When you hover over a commented cell, the comment will appear as below.

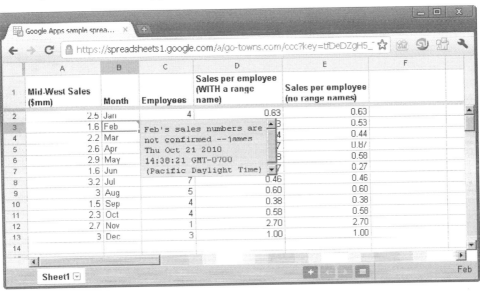

- **Chart/Gadget**: these are covered in detail shortly, but essentially are the shortcuts for embedding features that use your spreadsheet's data.

- **Image...**: this opens a dialog where you can enter the URL of an image you would like to use, or search for an image on Google Image search. Currently, there is no option to upload an image from your local computer, so you will need ensure the host is publicly hosted somewhere first.

- **Drawing**: you can add a Google Drawing to your spreadsheet using this option. The Drawing part of Docs is covered in chapter 9, and can be used to add headlines and graphical elements with more flexibility than using cell-based text or inserting images.

- **Script**: adds a script to the current spreadsheet, which is covered later in this chapter.

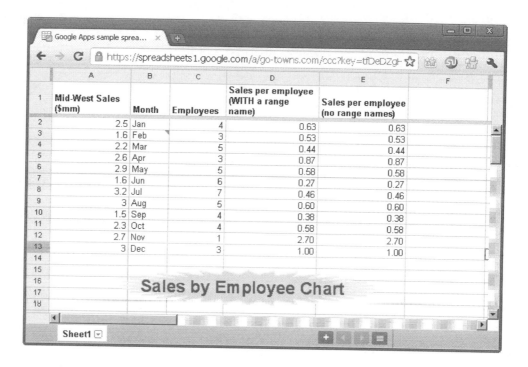

	Mid-West Sales ($mm)	Month	Employees	Sales per employee (WITH a range name)	Sales per employee (no range names)	
2	2.5	Jan	4	0.63	0.63	
3	1.6	Feb	3	0.53	0.53	
4	2.2	Mar	5	0.44	0.44	
5	2.6	Apr	3	0.87	0.87	
6	2.9	May	5	0.58	0.58	
7	1.6	Jun	6	0.27	0.27	
8	3.2	Jul	7	0.46	0.46	
9	3	Aug	5	0.60	0.60	
10	1.5	Sep	4	0.38	0.38	
11	2.3	Oct	4	0.58	0.58	
12	2.7	Nov	1	2.70	2.70	
13	3	Dec	3	1.00	1.00	

Sales by Employee Chart

The Format menu:

- **Format ▶ Font**: provides access to the range of browser-friendly fonts, not available in the toolbar. Currently there are six fonts to choose from.

- **Format ▶ Clear formatting**: this will remove any formatting from the current cell selection.

- **Format ▶ Change color with rules…**: a simple type of conditional formatting that will change the appearance of a cell based upon its contents. In the example on the next page, the *Sales per employee* values will turn yellow if they are greater than 0.75. You have the option to modify the appearance of the cell's text, background or both.

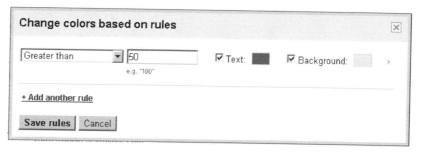

The Forms menu, between the Format and Tools menus, will be covered later in this chapter in detail, so has been omitted here.

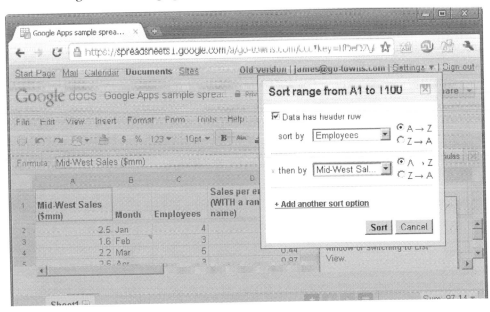

The Tools menu

- **Sort column A-Z/Z-A**: the first two choices allow you to sort the specific column in either ascending or descending order. If more than one column is selected, you have the choice of sorting by entire sheet or just the range.

- **Sort...**: if you need to sort based upon more than one criteria (e.g. sort on column C, then A, then B), this is the better option. After selecting the range that needs to be sorted, this feature will let you apply up to 10 levels of sort, with an ascending or descending option for each.

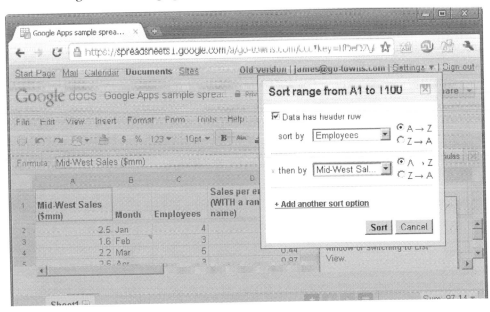

- **Freeze rows/columns**: the same as Excel's 'Freeze panes' – selected rows and columns remain static as the page is scrolled. Rows always remain fixed at the top of the sheet and columns remain fixed on the left. Frozen rows and columns will be excluded from sorting.

- **Check spelling**: lists cells with typographical errors (click **Previous** and **Next** to move between errors).

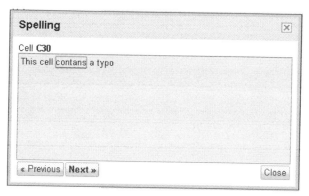

- **Protect sheet**: if you are working with other collaborators on a spreadsheet, this feature enables you to specify who is allowed to make edits. The default setting is everyone who has access, but it can be restricted to just the owner (you) or a specified list of users.

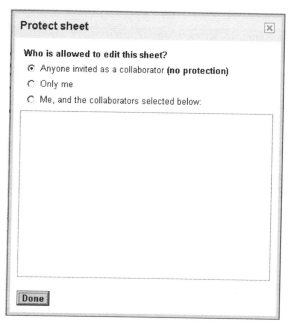

- **Set notification rules**: this is identical to the feature with the same name under the **Share** drop-down - see chapter 6 for details about notifications.

Data Validation

The next item on the tools menu provides a way to ensure that data in a cell meets some predefined criteria - click this item to open the data validation dialog box:

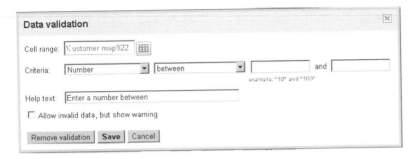

There are four parts to specify:

- **Cell range**: this is the target cell or cells that the rule will be applied to. Clicking the grid button allows you to select a cell range.

- **Criteria**: define the type of data (i.e. number, text, date or restricted list of items), and a rule that signals if the data entered is valid or not.

- **Help text**: this is a message shown to the user if their data is invalid.

- **Allow invalid data**: if this is checked, a warning will be displayed when invalid data is found. With it unchecked, the user will not be able to leave the cell until they provide valid data.

In addition to checking if number are within a certain range or text contains (or does not contain) a certain string of characters, you can use data validation to perform some useful tasks:

- Check that an email address or URL are valid. This doesn't check that the email exists or URL is correct - it just checks the formatting.

- Check that a date is valid (tests for entries like "02/30/2012"), or that a date is before or after some other date.

- Force the user to select from a list of items, and display a drop-drop next to the cell if required.

In this last case, the source for the drop-down can either be entered manually in this screen, or it can be driven by a range of cells on the spreadsheets. The latter option creates a dynamic way to validate data on your spreadsheet.

Formulas: the key to automating calculations

The real power of Spreadsheets lies in the ability to use formulas, which produce results based upon the data you provide. Any good spreadsheet application will have a wide range of formulas, making it possible to quickly calculate results, and also a good range of tracking tools to check the logic.

It's beyond the scope of this book to cover spreadsheets extensively, but their flexibility makes them ideal for a wide range of tasks, from running businesses to calculating your tax returns or household budget. In the simple example below, the spreadsheet automates the calculation of payroll based upon some simple formulas, so the result is:

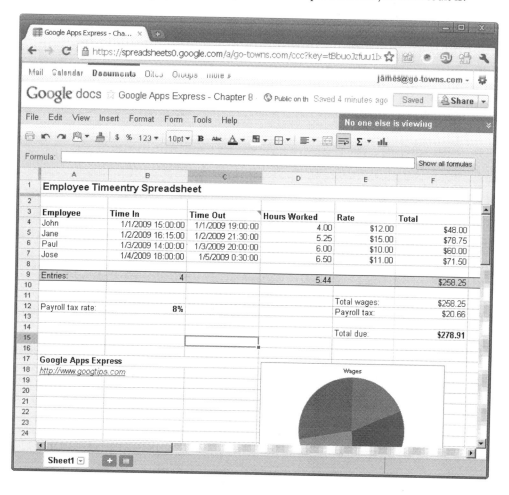

You can view this example at **http://goo.gl/ENUF6**. When all the formulas are displayed on this sheet (click **Show all formulas** on the formula bar), you can see how the example is put together. On the next page, let's look at how some of these basic formulas work.

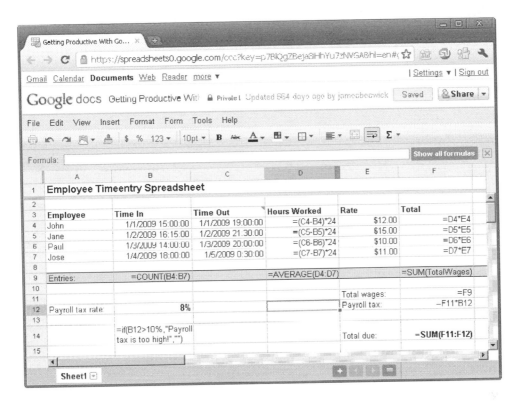

In this example, the spreadsheet calculates wages for four employees, based upon their working times entered in columns B and C, and their hourly rates in column E. Each formula is described below using the first row (4) as an example.

- **Hours worked (column D)**: by subtracting the start time (B) from the end time (C), this provides the fraction of the entire day worked. Multiply this fraction by 24 hours to show the result in hours. The formula is =**(C4-B4)*24**.

- **Total owed (column F)**: multiply the hours worked (D) by the rate per hour (E) and this shows the total. The formula is: =**D4*E4**.

- **The average hours worked (cell D9)**: this calculates the number of hours worked by each person divided by the number of people. The formula is =**Average(D4:D7)**, and uses a propriety function and a range.

- **The total wages (cell F9)**: the adds together the total hourly payroll for each employee. The formula is =**Sum(TotalWages)** but could also have been =**Sum(F4:F9)**. This uses a proprietary function and and a defined name range.

- **Payroll tax warning (cell B14)**: as a safeguard, this cell warns the user is the tax is over 10%. The formula is =**IF(B2>10%,"Payroll tax is too high!","")**. This tests if B2 is more than 10% using the IF function.

For each cell, you specify the value and it's format (number of decimal places, font, color, etc.) Actions can be performed against groups of cells by dragging the mouse pointer over the range you wish to change, and then selecting the appropriate action from the toolbar. Row heights and column widths are easily adjusted by dragging the divider lines between their names.

Many spreadsheet users don't use formulas, so they miss out on the most powerful part of spreadsheet applications. A formula can be as simple as **=10/2** and the cell will show '5' as the answer. Once a formula is in place, it will always show the most up-to-date value without you needing to recalculate. Cell F12 above has the simple formula **=F11*B12**, which guarantees a correct result whenever 'Total wages' or 'Payroll tax rate' changes.

Cell formulas are entered directly into cells, but they can also use functions which follow the convention of '**=FunctionName(Input data)**'. Each function yields a calculated result which will be placed in the same cell. In cell F14 above, the formula **=SUM(F11:F12)** tells Google Apps to add up the cells between F11 and F12 using the proprietary function **Sum**. If the values in either of those cells change, F14 will update automatically. Some of the most common formulas include:

- **Sum**: adds up a list of numbers (see F14).

- **Average**: provides the mean of a list of numbers (see D9).

- **Count**: counts the number of cells that contain a number (see B9).

- **If**: tests a condition and returns a value depending on if the condition is true or false.

Ranges are especially useful for functions, since a range could be thousands of cells. You specify a range in the format 'start cell:end cell' (e.g. D4:D7 includes D4, D5, D6 and D7 without needing to specify the two middle cells). While there's nothing wrong with entering =D4+D5+D6+D7 as a formula, =SUM(D4:D7) returns the same result and could be stretched to hundreds of cells easily (e.g. =SUM(D4:D700).

Formulas can also be nested, meaning their outputs can also be inputs for other formulas, resulting in cells such as D30 (**=if(sum(D4:D7)>30,"Too many hours","")**), which will sum the cells between D4 and D7 and show a warning if the total hours worked is over 30.

> Although this is convenient, nesting often leads to long formulas in cells that are overly complicated for users to read. It's easier to separate the steps into separate cells.

Named Ranges

Instead of referring to a range by it's not-so-friendly reference (e.g. A4:B7), you can assign the range a human-readable name. For example, I have two columns in the screenshot below called Sales (column A) and Employees (column C), and I want to calculate the sales per employee (in column D). I could easily enter the formula =A2*C2 in cell D2 and then fill down the formula for each row, but there's a more elegant solution with range names.

By clicking **Edit** ▶ **Named ranges** ▶ **Define new range...**, you can attach a nickname to a given cell range. Take a look at the example below, which is available at **http://goo.gl/X0M7R**. In this case:

- The range *sales* represents all of column A (known as A:A).

- The range *employees* is all of column C (known as C:C).

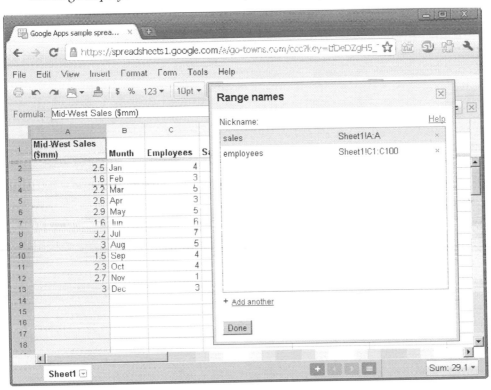

Now, for every cell in column D I can enter the formula **=sales/employees**. Google Spreadsheets is smart enough to figure out the rest, but more helpfully for anyone else reading the spreadsheet (or when I return several months after writing the spreadsheet), it's immediately clear what the formula means.

In column E, I've added the same formula without named ranges (e.g. =A2/C2) - as you can see, the results are the same as column D. So there's no difference in the calculation - it's simply a more maintainable way of handling spreadsheet contents.

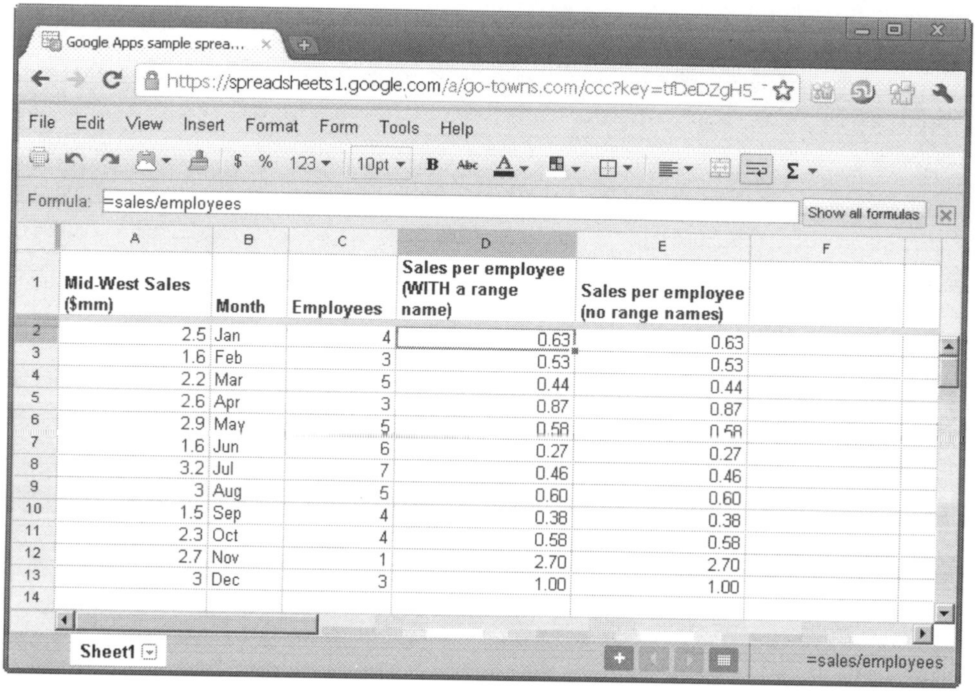

	A	B	C	D	E	F
1	Mid-West Sales ($mm)	Month	Employees	Sales per employee (WITH a range name)	Sales per employee (no range names)	
2	2.5	Jan	4	0.63	0.63	
3	1.6	Feb	3	0.53	0.53	
4	2.2	Mar	5	0.44	0.44	
5	2.6	Apr	3	0.87	0.87	
6	2.9	May	5	0.58	0.58	
7	1.6	Jun	6	0.27	0.27	
8	3.2	Jul	7	0.46	0.46	
9	3	Aug	5	0.60	0.60	
10	1.5	Sep	4	0.38	0.38	
11	2.3	Oct	4	0.58	0.58	
12	2.7	Nov	1	2.70	2.70	
13	3	Dec	3	1.00	1.00	
14						

Although the name implies that a named range should be a range of cells, it can also just represent a single cell. It's a useful technique for eradicating so-called "magic numbers" such as tax percentages that appear in formulas with no explanation. It's easier to read a formula referencing the name *default_tax_rate* than simply using the value 8.5%. And if several calculations use the value, changing the *default_tax_rate* cell will automatically update every calculation that uses it.

To make modifications to any existing named ranges, simply click **Edit ▶ Named ranges ▶ Manage ranges....** This screen allows you delete existing named ranges by clicking on the X next to the name, or update the cell range that each nickname represents.

Help with formulas

Entire books are written about spreadsheet functionality, and businesses use them extensively due to their massive computational ability. While there's significant overlap with the formulas available in Microsoft Excel, some behave slightly different while others are unique to Google Apps.

There are hundreds of built-in formulas, all of which you can view in a list by clicking on **Help ▶ Formula Builder...**:

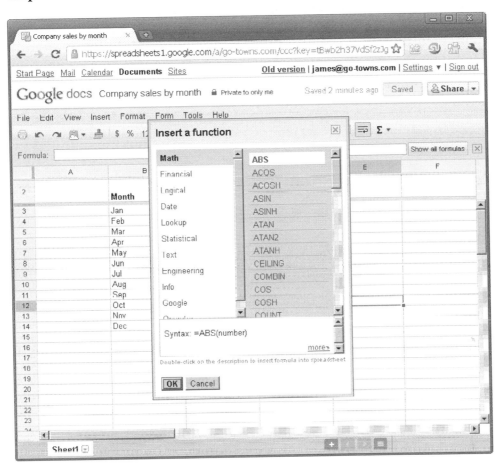

This shows a list of all the formulas supported by Google Apps, grouped by logical category, and a link to the help documentation for each function. Certain functions provide dynamic Internet search, such as *GoogleLookup*, which will try to find a result based upon an entity and attribute (see the example at **http://goo.gl/CnwSN**).

	A	B	C	D
	Formula: =googlelookup(A9,B9)			
1	**Entity**	**Attribute**	**Result**	
2	United Kingdom	Population	60943912	
3	France	Average age	39.1 years	
4	Germany	Population	82,282,988	
5	United States	Most expensive state	New York	
6				
7	John Travolta	Date of birth	February 18, 1954	
8	President Obama	Net worth	$10.5	
9	Velociraptor	Height	2.5 feet	
10			From: www.healthstones.com	
11			More options...	
12				

Scripts

If you've ever used the Visual Basic for Applications (VBA) programming language in Microsoft Excel, you'll know how powerful it is for customizing a spreadsheet to embed almost any sort of business logic that you need. Google Apps Scripts are written in JavaScript rather than VBA, but provide a similar level of flexibility allowing you to:

- **Link external data** to your spreadsheets: import from other Google Apps applications, connect with databases and send data to third party services.

- **Build spreadsheet functions**: while there's a large library of existing functions, you can now build functions designed specifically for your own business logic.

- **Automate time-consuming tasks**: scripts are good at doing simple, error prone jobs thousands of time, and can help improve your productivity.

- **Use other people's code**: many people release their scripts for the public gallery, so you can take advantage of their work without needing to understand code.

Using Third-Party Scripts

To use an existing script, click on **Insert ▶ Script** to open the Script Gallery:

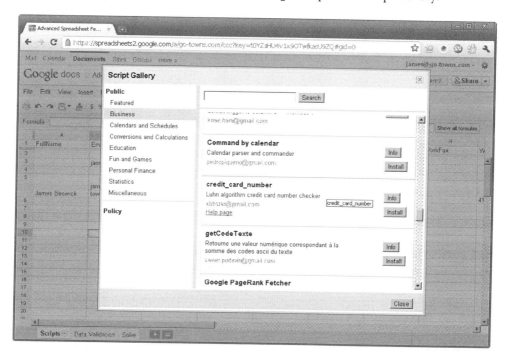

This window shows a listed of publicly-available scripts, grouped by category. As an example of how to use one of these, select the **Fun and games** group and find the script called 'EasterDate'. Before installing the script, click **Info** to see details about the author and what the script is designed to do, and then click **Install**.

You will see a request for authorization from Google Apps, asking for you to grant permission to the script. Just as with VBA or any scripting language, some scripts are malicious and should not be installed unless you trust the author or can verify that the code is not doing anything untoward. If you want to proceed, click **Authorize**.

This script adds a function called EasterDate, which takes a year as a parameter. Find an empty cell and type `=EasterDate(2012)`, and the cell will then display `2012-04-08`. See the spreadsheet at **http://goo.gl/1TMMR** for more details.

Managing Scripts

Once you have authorized one or more scripts in a spreadsheet, you can see these by clicking **Tools ▸ Scripts ▸ Manage**. The resulting dialog shows the list of new functions available, the script that owns the function, and any services that the code may be using (such as Google Calendar or Contacts).

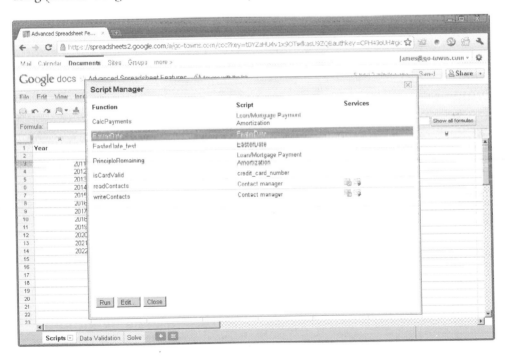

For functions with no parameters, you can run the script directly from this screen (it has no effect if parameters are needed). To see the code behind a function, select one and click **Edit...**.

181

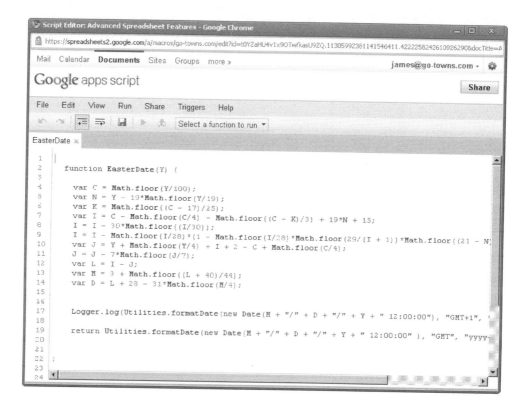

Here you can view the underlying JavaScript that powers the function. Just as with the VBA editor in Microsoft Excel, there are also debugging features such as breakpoints that enable the coder to see the state of the script at any given line of code.

Although scripting is beyond the scope of this book, there are some very useful options in Google Apps Script, including:

- The ability to set triggers (usually called events) that are custom to your functions, including time-based calls.

- Built-in error notification, so the creator will be automatically emailed if the script fails for some reason.

- Sharing and collaboration, allowing multiple coders to work on the same scripts.

- Publishing final code as a service to others on your domain.

Anyone in your organization with a basic understand of scripting will find it relatively easy to use Scripts. But if you don't have the skills in house to write something using Javascript, don't forget that the Google Marketplace is always available, where you can employ consultants and contractors to help you.

Using Widgets to bring your spreadsheets to life

You may have heard about gadgets, widgets, iframes and mash-ups – these are all relatively new features in the web 2.0 world. In web pages, you will often see small sections of Google Maps and other web applications residing within the page. These are useful additions to your site, since you harness the power of other applications or services without requiring the user to leave your page. Gadgets and widgets are designed to do just this, and they can be embedded in your spreadsheets in the same way to offer interesting new ways to present data and communicate with users.

From a Google Docs perspective, a gadget can be anything that uses and manipulates data on your spreadsheet to create something new – like charts, maps, pivot tables or visual representations of data. Unlike Excel, this opens the possibilities of merging your data with online services to produce something unique. And since users can write their own gadgets, the available library grows constantly.

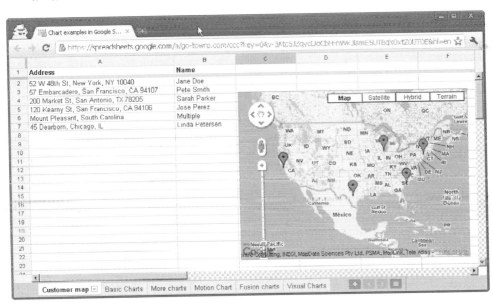

In the above example, the Google Maps gadget displays a list of customers visually across the United States. As new data is entered in columns A and B (location and customer name), a pushpin appears on the map. The map is interactive – it can be scrolled and zoomed just like a regular Google Maps display, and clicking on a pushpin will display the name of the customer.

All the charts in this section are available at http://goo.gl/Q7sKC.

Chart gadgets

From the spreadsheet view, click **Insert** ▶ **Gadgets** to view the entire library (**Insert** ▶ **Chart** only shows the most commonly used).

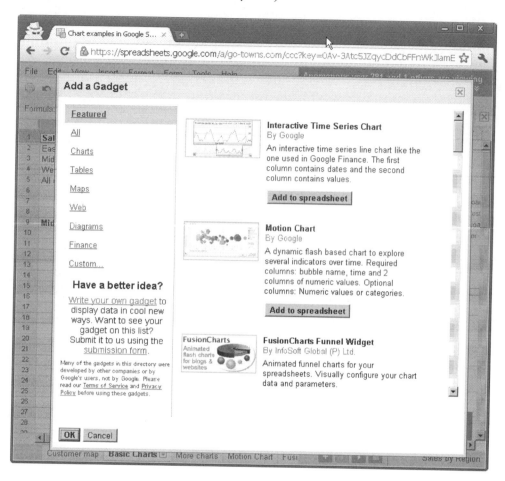

Click **Charts** to see all the charts commonly used in spreadsheet applications:

- **Pie chart**: shows % proportions as slices of a pie.

- **Bar chart**: shows data points by value.

- **Image line chart**: a line chart without visible values.

- **Area chart**: displays amounts over time.

- **Line chart**: display one or more data points as lines.

- **Scatter chart**: show data points as scatted dots on a chart.

- **Bar/column chart**: shows data in a bar or column format.

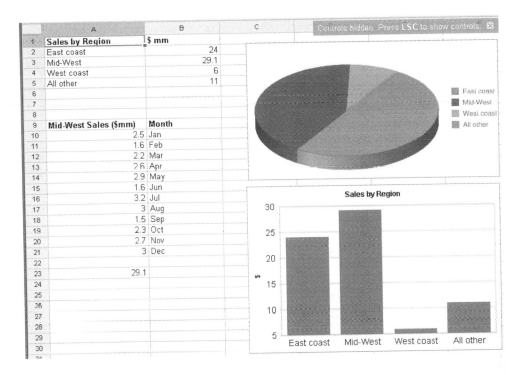

The basic sets of charts are less configurable than their Excel counterparts. The advanced charts offer ways to manipulate more series of data, or introduce animation and other controls into the gadget.

- **Timeline chart**: displays information on a user-configured timeline with access to individual images and events.

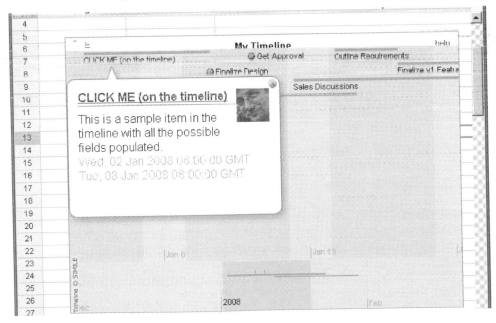

- **Interactive Time Series chart**: displays time versus value data, with optional events marked. Similar to the tool used in Google Finance to show company stock prices over a given period.

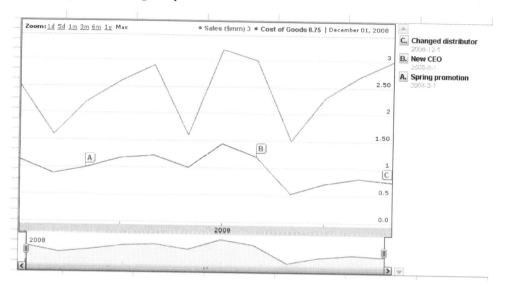

- **Motion chart**: a Flash-based gadget used for visually exploring the changes in several indicators over time.

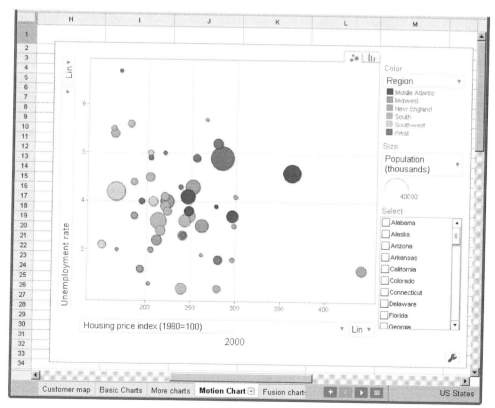

- **Fusion Charts**: animated versions of the pie chart and a funnel chart.

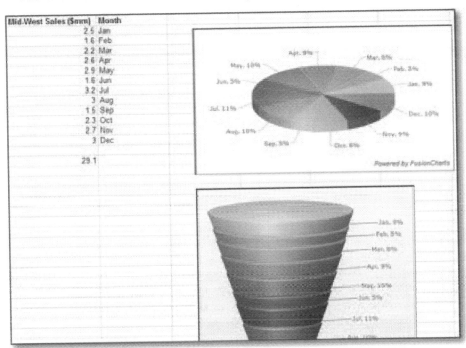

Visual charts represent data in unique ways, outside the core statistical ways of displaying information.

- **Gauges**: shows values on a gauge, with definable green, yellow and red 'safety areas'.

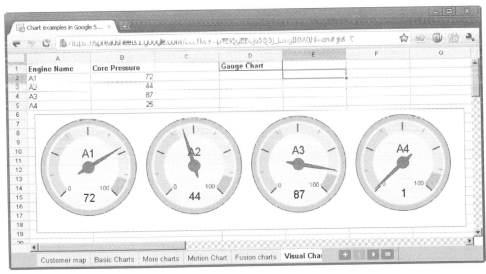

- **Gantt chart**: visualizes tasks on a Gantt timeline, enabling the user to select a time period and view percentage completion.

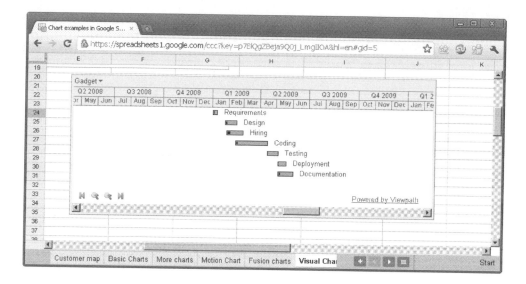

Table analytics are the Google equivalent of Excel's pivot tables, which create filtered and summarized views of flat data. For example, a flat table with individual sales transactions (see below), shows the detail of each sale but it's difficult to calculate sales by employee or category, or for a given month in this format.

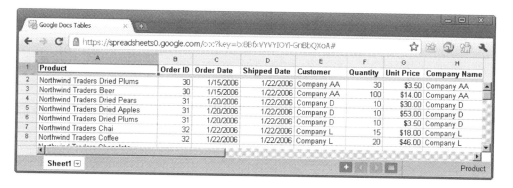

With a pivot table (shown on the next page), you specify the grouping column and filters (e.g. sales by category for March), and a new table is created that transforms the data.

Clicking the ➕ icon expands each grouping section to show the underlying detail. It's also possible to group on multiple columns, such as sales by category by employee.

Panorama Software also provides a pivot table widget called Analytics for Google Spreadsheets with even more features and chart formats. This widget uses a simple drag and drop approach (together with a video tutorial if you've never used pivot tables before).

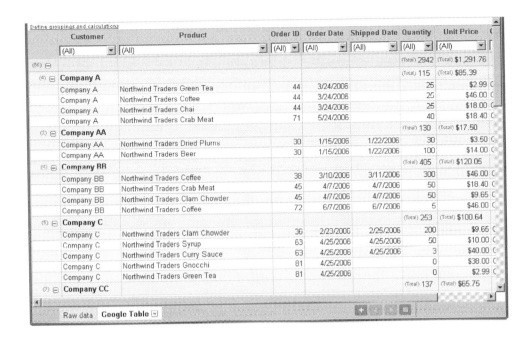

	Customer	Product	Order ID	Order Date	Shipped Date	Quantity	Unit Price	
	(All)	(All)	(All)	(All)	(All)	(All)	(All)	
(56)						(Total) 2942	(Total) $1,291.76	
(4) Company A						(Total) 115	(Total) $85.39	
	Company A	Northwind Traders Green Tea	44	3/24/2006		25	$2.99	C
	Company A	Northwind Traders Coffee	44	3/24/2006		25	$46.00	C
	Company A	Northwind Traders Chai	44	3/24/2006		25	$18.00	C
	Company A	Northwind Traders Crab Meat	71	5/24/2006		40	$18.40	C
(2) Company AA						(Total) 130	(Total) $17.50	
	Company AA	Northwind Traders Dried Plums	30	1/15/2006	1/22/2006	30	$3.50	C
	Company AA	Northwind Traders Beer	30	1/15/2006	1/22/2006	100	$14.00	C
(4) Company BB						(Total) 405	(Total) $120.05	
	Company BB	Northwind Traders Coffee	38	3/10/2006	3/11/2006	300	$46.00	C
	Company BB	Northwind Traders Crab Meat	45	4/7/2006	4/7/2006	50	$18.40	C
	Company BB	Northwind Traders Clam Chowder	45	4/7/2006	4/7/2006	50	$9.65	C
	Company BB	Northwind Traders Coffee	72	6/7/2006	6/7/2006	5	$46.00	C
(5) Company C						(Total) 253	(Total) $100.64	
	Company C	Northwind Traders Clam Chowder	36	2/23/2006	2/25/2006	200	$9.65	C
	Company C	Northwind Traders Syrup	63	4/25/2006	4/25/2006	50	$10.00	C
	Company C	Northwind Traders Curry Sauce	63	4/25/2006	4/25/2006	3	$40.00	C
	Company C	Northwind Traders Gnocchi	81	4/25/2006		0	$38.00	C
	Company C	Northwind Traders Green Tea	81	4/25/2006		0	$2.99	C
(7) Company CC						(Total) 137	(Total) $65.75	

Raw data   **Google Table** ▼

Other widgets: the best of the rest

Widgets are not limited to charts and analytics – conceptually they can take your spreadsheet data and transform it any way imaginable. Here are some of the others in the library that you can drop into Google Docs:

- **Heatmap**: displays a map with color intensities that match given values. The first column contains country ISO codes, and the other columns contain numeric values.

- **Translation**: translates from English contents to French, Spanish, Italian, German, Dutch, Portuguese, Japanese, Chinese, Korean, Russian or Arabic.

- **Word cloud**: displays text with words highlighted and enlarged based on their frequency in the source range of cells.

- **Web/image search**: returns Google results for terms in source cells, essentially an automated Google Search.

- **Organizational chart**: creates a hierarchy based upon employee and manager table values.

- **Money**: shows relative monetary values in piles of $100 bills.

- **Spreadsheet Mapper**: uses a combination of user-generated addresses and Google Maps to create a store locator, which could then be embedded on a corporate webpage.

Creating and configuring a gadget

When you select a gadget from the library, it will appear on the workbook with the settings dialog open. Although the exact settings vary between gadgets, certain options are universal. The simple bar chart settings (shown below) are standard for many gadgets.

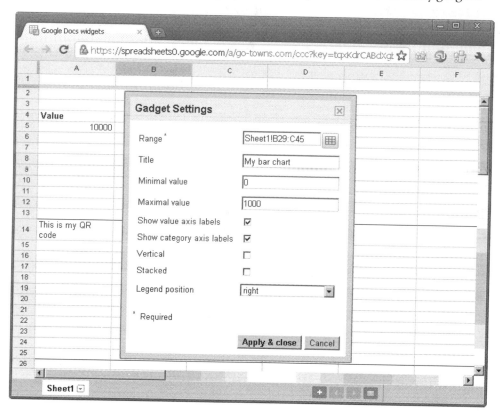

- **Range**: specify the source cells from the workbook. You can enter this in the format *WorksheetName!StartCell:EndCell* or – more easily – drag the range on the worksheet behind and this field will populate automatically.

- **Apply/Apply and close**: the first creates a preview of what the gadget will create – the second saves and closes the settings dialog.

- **Help**: some gadgets are more complicated than others, and may optionally provide additional help.

If you need to change the way a gadget is set up in the future, hover over its window and click **Edit Gadget...** in the top left, which will open the settings menu shown above. Learning how to use gadgets is easy but requires some experimentation, so you will find yourself changing these settings to get the exact result you need.

If a gadget isn't working out for any reason, you can remove it by clicking the drop-down arrow in the top left and selecting **Delete Gadget**. Since many gadgets are created by third-parties and have no support from Google, it's sometimes the case that they stop working. In the same drop-down, clicking **About this gadget...** will usually lead to a help page - but not always.

Gadgets: going beyond the spreadsheet

We've seen so far how you can add gadgets to spreadsheets and visualize data. But Google Apps takes things one step further, now that we're not tethered to desktop applications. How useful would it be to publish charts, maps and all the other features, so they could be viewed on web pages, emails or other documents without having to open a spreadsheet? For example, you could:

- **Send out an event invitation** using Google Forms and display a pie chart of who can attend on the event webpage.

- **Publish the results of customer feedback** on your web site.

- **Display sales statistics** on your internal web site.

- **Add your shopping list** to *iGoogle* so it's always available.

The first step is to click the drop-down on the top left corner of the gadget and select **Publish Gadget**, which creates a dialog box with a dozen or so lines of HTML.

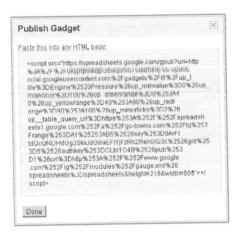

All you then need to do is cut and paste this HTML into a web page, and its results will then be visible on that page.

Alternatively, if you just want to add the Gadget to *iGoogle*, select that option from the same drop down. The next time you visit *iGoogle*, the gadget's contents will be visible:

Google Forms

The Google Forms application is one of the most unnoticed parts of Google Apps, but one of the most useful. It performs a complicated function very elegantly and is one of those features that's really appreciated when you realize it's there. It's build into the Google Spreadsheets application, and uses the spreadsheet as a data repository for the results.

Essentially, Forms is there any time you want to collect responses from a group of people. It provides a way of presenting questionnaire-style forms and collating all the results in a spreadsheet for further analysis. The reason why Forms is so useful is that gathering feedback like this has typically been awkward, usually requiring you to:

- **Send a mass-email** with the questions, and then search through the responses manually as they trickle back.

- **Create a proprietary web page** with custom programming to store responses in a database, which involves development time and cost.

- **Use a third-party service** like Survey Monkey to construct survey forms and compile results. Many of these services charge a fee above a certain number of recipients or questions.

With Forms, you can build surveys and questionnaires in minutes, distribute as easily as sending a URL, and then use the built-in analysis tools to visualize the resulting data. Although there are many potential uses, some of the most common include:

- **Customer surveys**: email a form to a customer list, allowing each recipient to complete a set of questions.

- **RSVPs for events**: automate the collection of responses from guests.

- **Internal suggestion programs**: create ad-hoc questions for friends and co-workers and collate their responses automatically.

There are several other major benefits of Google Forms:

- **Speed**: you can build questionnaires rapidly without any coding knowledge, and the form is available for distribution immediately.

- **Analysis**: Forms stores the responses in a spreadsheet, and provides additional reporting tools to visualize the data.

- **Security**: you can send out surveys securely by using https in the URL, meaning that nobody can eavesdrop on the data being collected.

- **No arbitrary limits**: you can create as many surveys as you need, with as many questions as you want, and send them to as many recipients as required.

- **Mobile-friendly**: just like any other part of Google Apps, Forms can be completed on smart phones and other mobile devices.

To access Forms, go to the Google Docs dashboard in your browser and click **Form ▶ Create Form**:

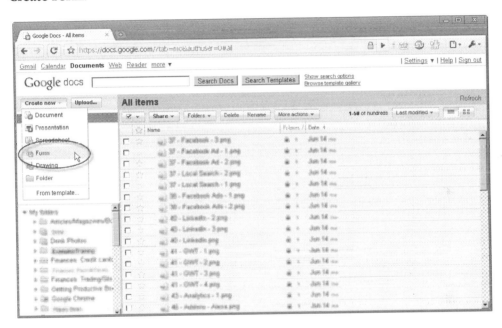

Creating your own forms

There are four main areas of the Forms interface (shown on the next page):

1. **Menu bar**: contains all the functions available in the form application, from setting the theme to visualizing the responses.

2. **Access options**: determine who can use the form and their access rights.

3. **Form editor**: where you build and edit the individual questions.

4. **Sharing URL**: this is the form's unique URL used for distribution.

Enter the name of your form and any instructions you want to provide in the first two text fields.

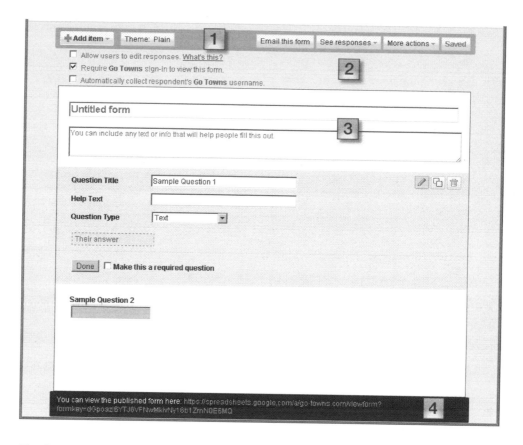

The functions should across the top of the page include:

- **Add item**: adds a new question to your form.

- **Theme**: select from nearly 100 defined themes to decorate your form.

- **Email this form**: sends an email with the form attached.

- **See responses ▶ Summary**: shows a graphical report of replies.

- **See responses ▶ Spreadsheet**: shows the data collected in the underlying spreadsheet.

- **More actions ▶ Embed**: generates the HTML needed to create an iframe on a webpage to display the form.

- **More actions ▶ Edit confirmation**: use for customizing the 'Thank you' text that a uses sees after submitting the form. You can optionally show a summary of responses to all users or just those in your domain.

The three checkboxes beneath enable users to edit previously-submitted forms, set the visibility of the form (everyone or just your domain), and collect user names.

Adding questions

Each question has a title and help text, which are both useful to clarify the response type from the user. You also need to decide the question format:

- **Text**: designed for questions that lead to short, freeform text responses (e.g. "What's your name?").

- **Paragraph text**: allows a longer freeform response for questions expecting more feedback (e.g. "What's the best part of our service?").

- **Multiple choice**: used when the answer is restricted to one out of a range of possible values (e.g. "What's your favorite type of car?"). You also have the option of adding "Other", allowing the user to enter a response outside of the predefined list.

- **Checkboxes**: enables several responses to a question (e.g. "Which days of the week do you drive to work?"). Typically, this works best for questions where you might add 'check all that apply'.

- **Choose from a list**: for selecting a single value from a drop-down of possible options (e.g. "What's your month of birth?").

- **Scale (1-n)**: for quantitative responses where the user is required to enter a number between two values (e.g. "How would you rate our service from 1-10?").

- **Grid**: used to create a table of items, where the thing to be measured is shown in the rows, and acceptable answers are shown in the columns.

With each question, you can also make a response required by selecting the checkbox. Once you have defined a question, click **Done** to save. The icons in the top right of the question box allow you to edit, duplicate or delete a question (duplicating is useful in case you have similar questions).

If you need to change the order of questions, drag and drop the question boxes into the preferred position. Once completed, the URL for your form is shown in the black box at the base of the window (which is easy to miss). Click **Save** when you are finished.

Each question corresponds to a column in the underlying spreadsheet. Although your questionnaire is publicly viewable, the spreadsheet's visibility is not unless you explicitly change this setting.

An online survey for this book demonstrating every question type is at http://goo.gl/O7Xm9 and appears on the next page.

Google Apps Express - Reader Survey

Please provide feedback and we'll incorporate your suggestions into our next edition. If you provide your email, we will send you a link with discounts for future versions. Thanks for your time!

Your name *

→ **Text**

Your email address
(We don't sell or distribute your email.)

How are you intending to use Google Apps?
Tell us a little about your interest in the Apps platform.

Paragraph text

Where do you normally go for technical advice? *

- ○ Books
- ○ Online help groups
- ○ Friends and colleagues
- ○ Experimentation
- ○ Other:

Multiple choice

In the last six months, which book formats have you purchased? *

- ☐ Printed book (hardback, softback, etc.)
- ☐ Downloadable PDF
- ☐ Kindle version
- ☐ Other:

Checkboxes

How many people are you deploying Google Apps to? *

Individual ▼

Choose from a list

How would you rate each chapter?
(1 is poor, 5 is excellent)

	1	2	3	4	5
Chapter 1	○	○	○	○	○
Chapter 2	○	○	○	○	○
Chapter 3	○	○	○	○	○
Chapter 4	○	○	○	○	○
Chapter 5	○	○	○	○	○
Chapter 6	○	○	○	○	○
Chapter 7	○	○	○	○	○
Chapter 8	○	○	○	○	○
Chapter 9	○	○	○	○	○
Chapter 10	○	○	○	○	○

Grid

Overall, how would you rate this book? *
1 is poor; 10 is excellent

	1	2	3	4	5	6	7	8	9	10	
Poor	○	○	○	○	○	○	○	○	○	○	Excellent

Scale (1-n)

Other form options

After the user submits the form, a confirmation page is shown with a generic message. You can edit this message by clicking **More Actions ▶ Edit confirmation**.

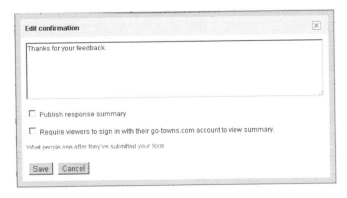

Your user form can be distributed by email using the URL link provided, or it can be embedded into a webpage. Embedding sounds complicated, but selecting **More Actions ▶ Embed** generates all the HTML code that's needed, which looks like this:

```
<iframe src="https://spreadsheets.google.
com/embeddedform?key=0123456789" width="310"
height="1299" frameborder="0" marginheight="0"
marginwidth="0">Loading...</iframe>
```

Dropping this snippet into any HTML editor will place your survey on a webpage – the functionality is exactly the same, but you can control the appearance of the areas around the form.

Handling results

As mentioned, when users complete your online survey, the results are stored in a Google spreadsheet. There are two ways to review the responses:

- **Summary**: to view the summary, click **Form ▶ Show summary** and a window will appear graphically depicting the feedback.

- **Raw data**: the raw data is stored with each spreadsheet column representing responses from a question.

If you want to receive an email each time a response is entered, simply change the notification settings in the spreadsheet (go to **Share ▶ Set Notification Rules**) and you can opt for a real-time email or a daily summary. If you want to suspend the form, uncheck **Form ▶ Accepting responses**.

Frequently Asked Questions

Q. What's the maximum size of a spreadsheet.

Spreadsheets must be under 256 columns and 400,000 cells, with a maximum of 40,000 cells with formulas. Uploaded spreadsheets must be under 20 Mb (and must meet the column and cell restrictions).

Q. How many collaborators can view a spreadsheet?

You can collaborate with as many people as you choose, but real-time sharing is limited to 50 simultaneous users.

Q. How can I access my spreadsheet or form securely?

Both spreadsheets and forms are accessed through a URL – to ensure secure access, change the **http://** at the beginning to **https://**. You can set https as the default in your Google account settings.

Q. Why does the printing look messy?

You have to print from within the Google Docs application, not from the browser itself. Go to **File ▶ Print** for a clean version of your sheet. You can also export to PDF, XLS and CSV from the Export submenu.

Q. Is it safe to use scripts?

Not always. As with any embedded scripting language (like VBA), there's a chance that a script is doing something malicious. To be safe, only run scripts from trusted sources.

Q. How can I make changes to the sheet name or add a new sheet?

Each document can contain multiple worksheets – by default, one is created when you start a new document, called Sheet1. This can be renamed by clicking the drop-drown arrow next to the name, and clicking **Rename**. It can also be deleted or duplicated from the same menu. If you want to add a blank new sheet, just click the **Add Sheet** button at the bottom of the screen.

Q. The form URL is too long - is there a way to make it shorter?

The easiest way is to use a URL shortening service such as **http://bit.ly** or **http://goo.gl** since the form's URL's is automatically generated. Some of these services, such as goo.gl, will provide additional statistics to show how many visitors clicked through the link.

9. Google Presentations

The Google Presentations component is one of the latest additions to the suite, though the least developed when compared with its Microsoft Office counterpart. PowerPoint has developed since its inception to become the premier presentation software in the business environment, with a host of display and animation options that are largely missing from Google Presentations.

But don't let that deter you. The Presentations piece still enables you to assemble decks of slides rapidly, edited collaboratively in real time, and published online with no software required. It also allows PowerPoint presentations (PPT files) to be imported and manipulated, making it easy to take more complex PowerPoint documents and view remotely without having to send files around.

As with the other Google Docs applications, power users of the Microsoft alternative will likely embrace both platforms to some extent, while users wanting the simpler features will find the Google Apps approach refreshingly easy and quick to adopt.

As an aside, I would expect major developments in Google Presentations over the next year or so, especially given the capabilities of HTML5, which could ultimately lead to a product with more impressive animation and presentation capabilities than PowerPoint.

To load Google Presentiations, open **http://docs.google.com** in your browser and log in, or click the **Documents** heading from any Google service to bring you to the common Documents interface.

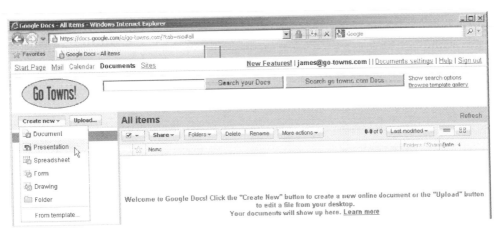

From here, click **Create new ▶ Presentation** to open the application.

A quick tour of the Presentations Interface

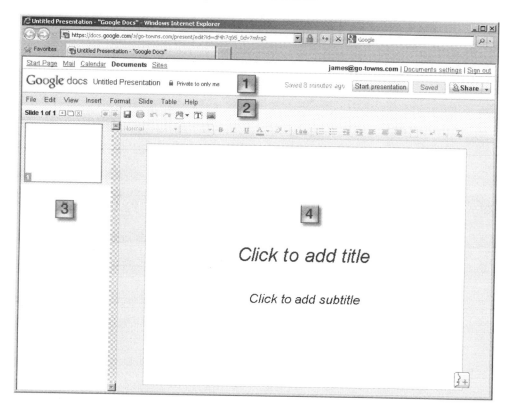

There are four main parts of the Google Presentations interface:

1. **Header**: the name of the document, sharing options, a link back to Docs, help and account options are shown across the top.

2. **Menus**: as with PowerPoint, most presentation functions are organized here, split between drop-down menus and a toolbar.

3. **Slides**: these are organized vertically – clicking any slide will open it for editing.

4. **Slide editor**: the main workspace where slide content is created and changed.

A presentation is a collection of slides, which are then seen by the audience as a locked-down show in a sequence that you decide. Consequently, there are two modes in Presentations – the 'design time' mode, where you build and order the slides, and the 'run time' mode which plays your finished deck.

Using Themes

The default view of a new presentation is one blank slide with two generic title boxes. It's based on a fixed theme called Blank. If you want to change to a predefined theme that's a little more interesting, click **Format ▶ Presentation Settings ▶ Change theme**:

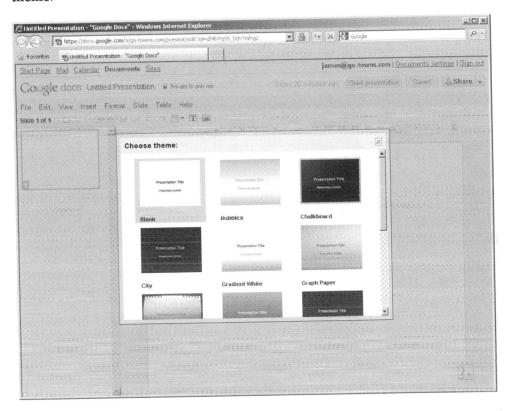

Selecting one of the options changes the background, default fonts and colors, and you'll immediately see your blank presentation updated. These themes are somewhat limiting, but fortunately you can also import any of the thousands of Powerpoint templates available on the web.

To use a PowerPoint template, you can either choose one of the templates included in Office or Office Online, or search the web for PowerPoint templates. Once you have located the pot or potx file you want to use, open the file in PowerPoint. Click **File ▶ Save As...** and save the file as type ppt.

Since Google Docs will not currently handle pptx or potx file formats, this step converts the document into the ppt extension that it can read and convert to a Google Docs document. Next, click **Upload** from the Google Docs main window, or click **File ▶ Upload** from Google Presentations.

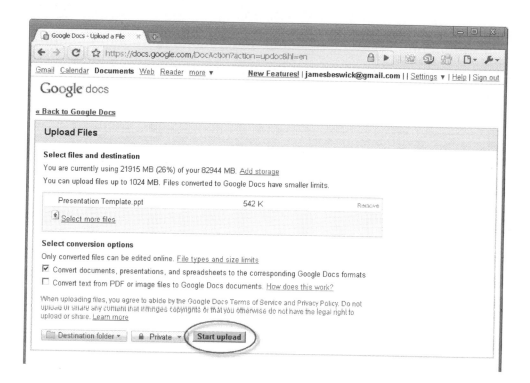

Click **Select files to upload** and select the ppt file you just saved. Afterwards, click **Start upload**, ensuring the first option to convert the file to Google Docs is checked.

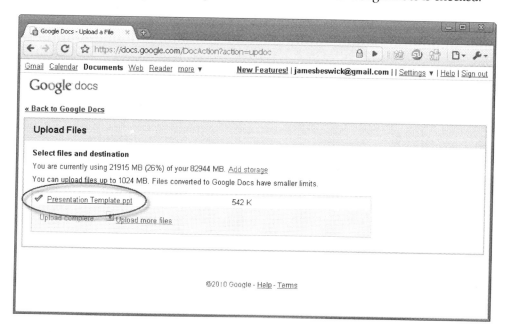

Once uploaded, click the hyperlinked filename to open the template. This is how the ppt file appears in PowerPoint and Google Apps:

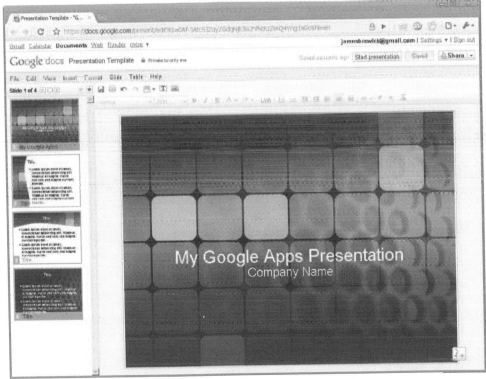

Creating and editing slides

To create a brand new slide, click **Slide** ▶ **New** slide (or press Control + M). If you want to duplicate an existing slide, select **Slide** ▶ **Duplicate** slide instead (useful if your slides have similar layout and graphics).

An individual slide has four different types of item that can be added and changed – you can choose one or several to use from the Insert menu:

- **Text**: places a box on the slide that can contain text.

- **Image**: places an image on the page, which can be uploaded from your computer or network, or an existing image on the Internet.

- **Video**: embeds a video player into the presentation, with the limitation that the video must be hosted on YouTube. Since YouTube is a public system, this means you should not host private or sensitive company materials there. Currently, there is no way to embed a private video.

- **Shape**: there are 12 shapes available, from squares and circles to arrows and speech bubbles.

When you select one of these object types, it will be placed in the middle of the current slide within a bounding box. The bounding box defines the positioning and scale of the item. To change its position, move the mouse over the edge lines and drag; to change its size, select one of the squares around the box and drag. For text boxes, the width defines where word-wrapping will occur.

When you add an object, it's automatically inserted on the top-most layer. If you are working with several objects, such as text inside a speech bubble, or a circle around an image, you will be placing layers on top of each other. When one layer is on top, it blocks out the layer beneath it, so there is a three-dimensional order to the objects you place on the slide (see above)

For example, here are three objects placed on a slide and how they will look in the final presentation: The layer order isn't immediately visible, but from a three-dimension perspective would look like this:

1. **Slide background**: this is always the deepest layer.

2. **Image**: the apple image appears between the background and layer 3.

3. **Shape**: the circle shape overlays the image beneath.

4. **Textbox**: the text appears on top of all other layers.

Most of the time this happens unnoticeably, but there are times when an object blocks the view of another, and you want to push it further towards the background, or bring another in front. The way to do this is to right-click the object you wish to move and select one of the following options:

-   **Bring to front**: moves the object to the front (from the viewer's perspective).

-   **Send to back**: pushes the objects back to the background.

-   **Bring forward**: brings the item one layer forward towards the viewer.

-   **Send backward**: sends the item one layer towards the background.

-   **Flip horizontal/vertical**: this doesn't affect the layer order, but transforms shapes. Flipping cannot be performed on text or images.

These options are also available in the **Arrange** menu after you select an item.

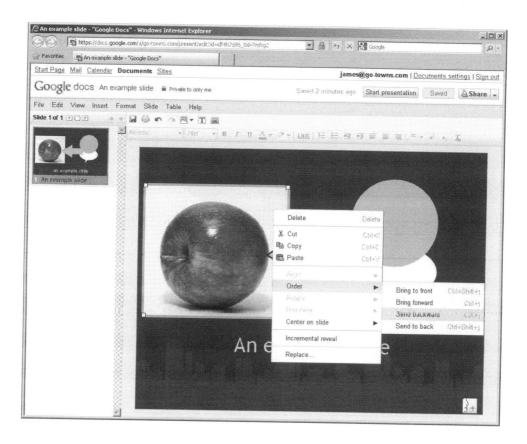

In addition to these four different types of content, there are two others: the background, and speaker notes.

To change the background, click **Format ▶ Presentation settings ▶ Change background**. You can select either a solid color or a custom image from your computer, and choose whether it affects only the current slide or all the slides in a presentation.

Speaker notes (see opposite) can be turned on and off by clicking the icon in the bottom-right hand corner of the screen – when enabled, a pane will open on the right-hand side. Speaker notes do not appear as part of the presentation but they provide an aid for the presenter to indicate which points relate to a given slide - and a great way to avoid simply reading slides to an audience.

Once you have a list of slides, changing the order is as simple as dragging the slides around in the left-most column. There are also options to move slides up and down by right-clicking the appropriate slide and selecting the desired option from the subsequent menu.

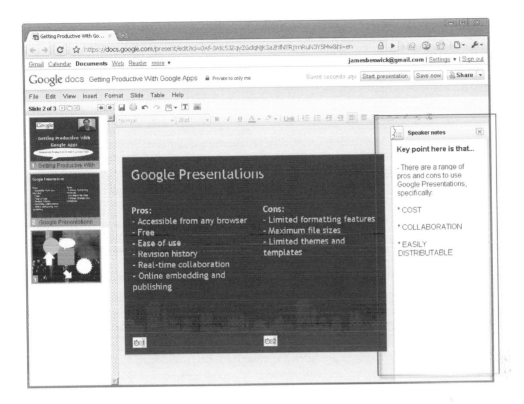

Deleting slides and revision history

If you need to remove a slide, click **Slide ▶ Delete**. This permanently removes it from the presentation, although it is still recoverable by undoing immediately after (**Edit ▶ Undo** or **Ctrl** + Z).

Just as with the other Google Apps, Presentations remembers all the changes ever made to a document. If you have made changes that you need to recover, go to **File ▶ Revision History**. Revisions are numbered and dated, with a basic description of the change, and you simply need to click a version to revert back.

Minor changes are grouped together on the right (click to expand these). Selecting a revision will show what the presentation looked like at that point – if you want to rewind back to the version, click **Revert to this version** at the top. When you revert back, you will lose any changes made since that revision.

Presenting to the audience

Click **Start Presentation** to walk through the slides and a new browser window appears in full screen mode. You can move between slides by pressing the arrows in the bottom left (or using the cursor keys to move backwards and forwards).

Click **View speaker** notes to see the notes for your presentation, which will open in a separate window and remain synchronized as you move through the slides.

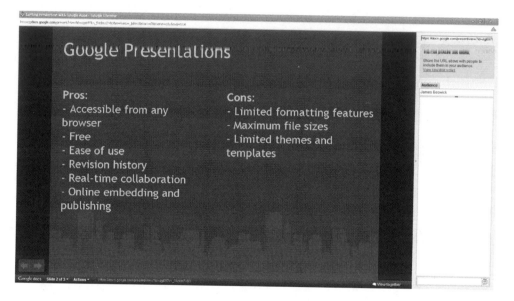

If your audience is viewing on separate browsers, they can send messages to the group by entering comments and clicking on the smiley face icon. Viewers only need the URL of the presentation in order to view.

The toolbar at the bottom of the window allows you to print, download and edit slides, and also provides the URL needed for others to view your presentation. Unlike Power-Point, you can distribute this URL to anyone who has a browser and Internet access and they will be able to view the slides without any additional software (this includes smart phone users).

You can view this sample presentation at http://goo.gl/UcUDD.

Google Drawings

Google Drawings lets create and collaborate on drawings for use in other Google Apps applications. With Drawings you can insert text, shapes, lines and images from your computer, and then use the layout tools to position these on the canvas.

Drawings can be created as standalone documents or embedded in spreadsheets, documents and presentations.

- To create a new drawing from scratch, visit your Google Docs explorer and click **Create new ▶ Drawing** to load the application.

- To draw directly in Google Presentations, go to **Insert ▶ Drawing**.

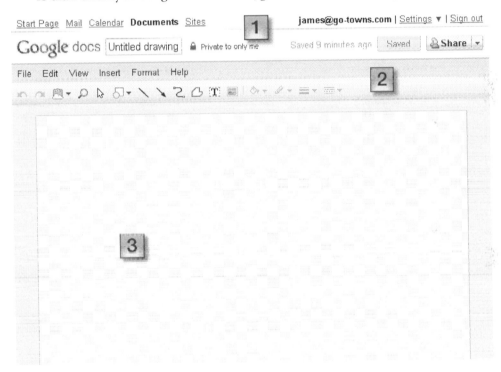

There are three main areas on the screen:

1. **Header**: as usual, this contains the application links, settings, sharing and saving options, and the name of the drawing.

2. **Menu and toolbar**: all the main functions of the drawing application are here.

3. **Canvas**: the workspace area for your drawing.

The Drawing toolbar

The toolbar contains the following functions (from left to right):

- **Undo/Redo**: backtrack on the latest sequence of changes or reapply if needed.

- **Web clipboard**: copies the current selection to a Google-hosted clipboard. Unlike the Windows clipboard, this allows multiple items to be stored simultaneously, and allows efficient pasting between different computers and applications. The web clipboard follows the logged-in user from browser to browser.

- **Zoom**: click to change the mouse pointer to a magnifying glass - clicking anywhere on the canvas will zoom into that area.

- **Selection arrow**: click to change the mouse pointer to the selection arrow, which allows you to select one or more elements on the canvas.

- **Insert shape**: click to show a drop-down with a list of predefined shapes:

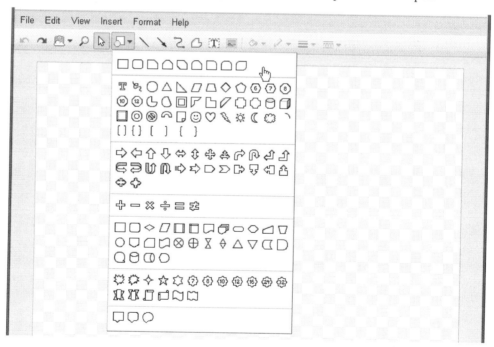

- **Line/arrow**: insert a line or arrow by clicking the start and end points on the canvas. When you select the line, there are four more options that appear on the toolbar, allowing you change the line's weight, style and arrowhead type on each end:

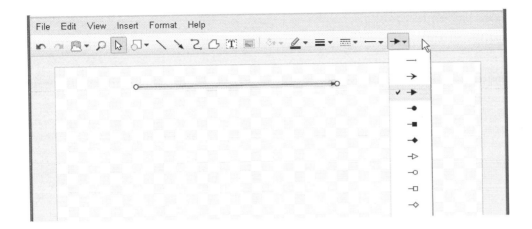

- **Curve**: creates a Bezier curve shape on the canvas, with each click adding an additional curve. Press **Esc** to stop drawing. To modify the points along the curve, right click and select **Edit Points**:

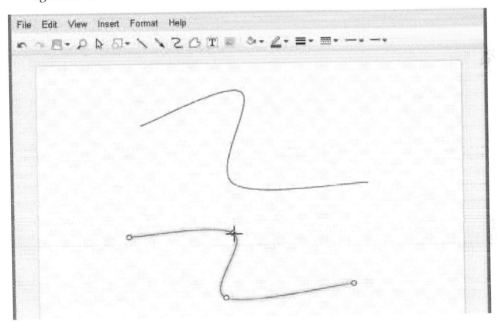

- **Polyline**: use this to draw a shape consisting of several lines. Click back at the first point to close and fill the shape, or press **Esc** to leave the shape open.

- **Text**: use to add text to your drawing (press **Shift**+**Enter** for multiple lines). When you select a text box, six new items appear on the toolbar enabling you to edit the text, applying bold, italic, coloring, justification and font size respectively.

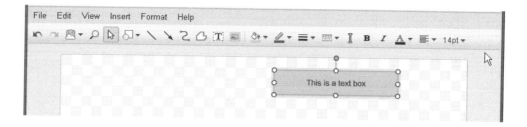

- **Insert image**: this option can add an image from your local computer, a public URL or from Google Image Search. It's the same image dialog used in other Google Docs applications.

- **Background fill**: click to add a background color to your shapes.

- **Pen color**: change the line color of the selected shape.

The Drawing menu options

Many of the drawing menu options repeat features on the toolbar but the key differences are:

- **File ▶ Download as**: you can download the drawing in PNG, JPEG, SVG or PDF format.

- **View**: allow you to change the scale of the canvas, and zoom in or out.

- **Insert**: repeats many of the features of the toolbar, except for Arc, Word Art, and scribble. Word Art is essentially a text box with the ability to change the font within a limited range.

You can view a sample Google Drawing at http://goo.gl/ABVKf.

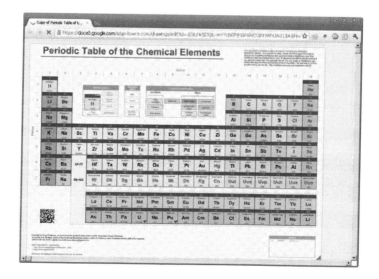

Advanced Features

Sharing and collaboration

One of the real annoyances of PowerPoint is trying to compile feedback from other users to build a presentation into a final version. This can be substantially more complex than the same exercise with Word or Excel, since many changes are not noticeable, such as animations and speaker notes, and others affect the whole document, such as modifications to the master slides.

This area is a real strength of Google Presentations, since all changes are added to the document in real time, so all users can immediately see updates and collaborate together. To enable this, click the **Share** drop-down, and then **Sharing settings**.

The familiar sharing screen appears – enter the email addresses of those you wish to invite, and then decide if they can edit (with full access) or only view (read-only). As in other Google Apps, you can also review and remove permissions from existing collaborators on this screen.

As usual, you have the option to send an email notification to any new collaborators, and you can define whether they are also allowed to invite people and modify permissions (see chapter 6 for more on sharing).

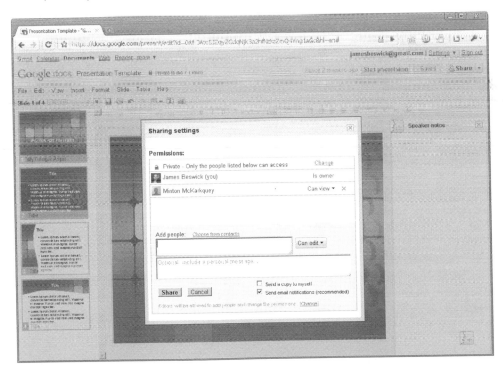

Embedding presentations

Click the **Share** drop-down and select **Publish/Embed** to publish your presentation to the world - this leads to a wizard that creates the HTML code needed to embed your document. As always, embedding occurs using iframes (internal frames), which sound complicated but actually require no more than cut-and-paste.

1. Click **Publish Document** to start the process. If you selected the wrong document or change your mind, click Stop Publishing in the subsequent screen to return to this first page.

2. Google Apps provides the URL needed to access the presentation. If you only want to share the URL to an audience, you can stop at this stage.

3. If you'd like to embed the presentation in a webpage, select your preferred presentation size and player options (such as timing between each slide)

4. Copy the HTML code to the clipboard (highlight and press CTRL + C).

The embed code will look like this, although some parameters will be different:

```
<iframe src="https://docs.google.com/present/
embed?id=XXXXX&autoStart=true" frameborder="0"
width="410" height="342"></iframe>
```

This can be pasted into the HTML of a webpage to show the presentation. There are a variety of HTML editors available, such as Dreamweaver, Expression Web and free software such as Page Breeze, and you can even write HTML in any text editor.

A quick embedding example

To show you how simple embedding is, let's create an embedded presentation using Notepad (click **Start** ▶ **Run**, type **Notepad** and press Enter).

When Notepad loads, enter the following text:

```
<head></head><body>
This is my webpage.<br/><br/>
</body></html>
```

Double-check your spelling carefully, since in HTML punctuation really does matter. Click **File** ▶ **Save As...** and store the file with the name **C:\Test.HTML** (make sure the **Save As type** drop-down is 'All Files' or Windows will add *txt* to the file name).

To see the how this basic web page will appear, open your favorite browser and enter **c:\ test.html** as the address   you will see a blank page with the line 'This is my webpage'.

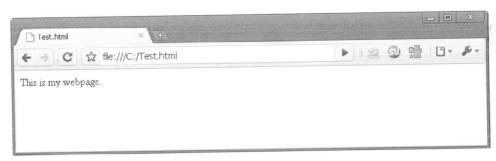

Now let's add the presentation. With the HTML on the clipboard, go back to Notepad. Between the line <br/> and </body>, paste the code from the Google embed window so that your new file looks like this:

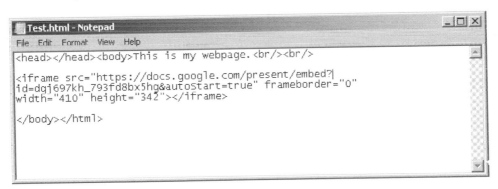

Save the file and return to your browser. Reload or refresh the web page and the presentation will appear embedded below the line of text.

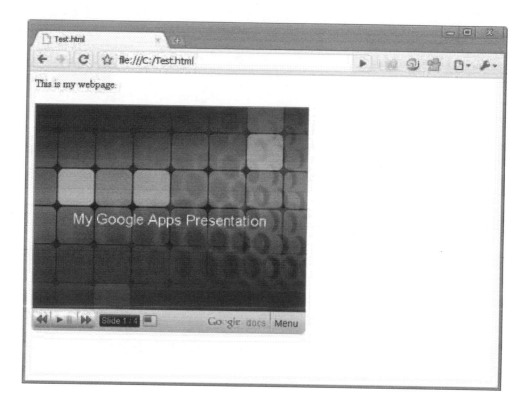

While this is a very basic embedding example, it demonstrates how you can cut and paste the HTML to include a complex presentation only with the code provided. The presentation can be just as easily added to your company's webpage or blog - or any other HTML page.

The embedded presentation player has its own set of controls that allow the user to move between slides, or launch the document into a new window. These controls always appear and cannot be customized. If you need to change the width and height to something other than the size defaults provided, simply edit the values in the HTML.

Importing presentations

There are three main reasons to upload from the desktop to Google Apps:

- You are migrating to Google Apps and need to move your files.

- You have produced a presentation with PowerPoint and want to distribute the content on the Internet.

- You have produced a presentation with PowerPoint and want to collaborate with colleagues in real time, or edit with someone who does not have PowerPoint installed.

First, the uploading process does not accept the new Office 2007 pptx format – any presentation must be saved in PowerPoint as the older ppt format. Once you have a ppt file ready for upload, the next limitation is that it must be under 10 MB (you will receive an error if you try to exceed this size).

Uploading is simple: click Upload from the main Google Docs windows, or **File ▶ Upload a presentation...** from the presentation view. Select the ppt file and click the Upload File button.

The conversion process does not create an identical copy of the presentation in terms of appearance – you will lose all animations and slide transitions, macros, and other complex features. Any text boxes in PowerPoint with special graphic effects or SmartArt objects will be flattened into static pictures that look the same in Google, but can no longer be edited.

Essentially, Google translates the original ppt file to be consistent with the features supported in Google Presentations – depending on the complexity of your PowerPoint original, the Google version may look identical or be considerably different.

Frequently Asked Questions

Is any animation supported?

Yes, but only one – an Incremental Reveal, which is available on the right-click menu of an object. This is the same as PowerPoint's Fade In option. If several objects use Incremental Reveal, the right click option allows you to change the order of appearance.

Can I embed widgets like in other Docs applications?

No, Google Presentations does not currently support widgets. I suspect this is likely to change since widgets are one of the most useful features of Docs and logically would make Google Presentations differentiated from PowerPoint.

Can I import Microsoft PowerPoint templates?

Strictly, no, but if you change the file extension from pot to ppt, it will upload as a regular PowerPoint file.

10. Google Sites

There's some confusion around what the Google Sites product really is, so let's examine what it is and what it is not. It's not:

- A competitor to Dreamweaver, WordPress, FrontPage, Expression Web or any other web design product. It doesn't allow enough customization or scripting to make it nearly as powerful as any of these tools.

- A basic website development platform like Weebly - there are limits to what Google Sites will let you do.

- A replacement for your company's existing website, which may have all sort of complexity and custom design, none of which is very easy in Google Sites.

But don't get discouraged, because there are many uses outside of the obvious use for corporate websites. It is:

- Capable of average levels of web design in a very short space of time - arranging pages, files and permission within minutes is well beyond standard web platforms.

- A replacement for the Google Page Creator product: Google has now basically retired this. If you don't know about Page Creator, don't worry since the best parts are in Google Sites.

- A platform for creating structured and dynamic web pages: this is the key thing, since most of us now want web pages that are more than just static billboards.

All of this confusion would probably disappear if the product were renamed Google Wiki, since the tool performs more like a Wiki than a major Content Management System or website platform.

So just what is a Wiki? You may have used Wikipedia, the popular online encyclopedia. Apart from being freely accessible and very large, the really unique feature is that content is read, written, deleted and managed by its members. Unlike a magazine or book, where contributors have work controlled and approved by editors, and readers can only consume the result, a Wiki flattens the hierarchy and makes everyone a potential reader, writer and editor.

> **Wiki is a Hawaiian word for 'fast' but is also rumored to be an acronym for 'what I know is'.**

221

The reason why wikis are so powerful is they allow a loosely structured and highly flexible environment for collaboration. As with all Google Apps, the location of each member of a wiki group is irrelevant, and Sites provides a basic framework for members to add and review information.

A site can also include content from Google Docs, files and external services, adding a dynamic element to the content. As we'll see, building a Google Site takes minutes, and can be used for some fairly sophisticated tasks that would otherwise require custom coding.

Why would this be useful to your organization? As examples, Sites could be used to:

- Build a company's Human Resources intranet page, including forms and documents for employees and new hires, and a discussion forum for HR personnel.

- Manage a Baseball League, with profiles of all the players and a match history, and videos of every game.

- Collaborate on team projects, from arranging a birthday party to building a house, or even getting a President elected.

- Operate as a file server for a charitable organization, enabling users to share files and maintain version history.

The possible uses in real life are limitless – any situation that requires information sharing across a group of people is an ideal application. Sites can draw together news resources, company documents, calendars, photographs announcements and links.

Once you have created a Google Apps, you can access Google Sites by opening a browser and visiting either:

- **http://sites.mydomain.com**: if you set a custom URL for the service (see chapter 2), you can access the site on your own sub-domain.

- **http://sites.google.com/a/yourdomain.com**, replacing *yourdomain* with your actual domain name. This is the default URL that will always work even if you have set up a shortcut sub-domain.

Alternatively, if you are logged into another Google Apps service such as Gmail, you can reach Google Sites using the application links at the top of the page.

Starting a site

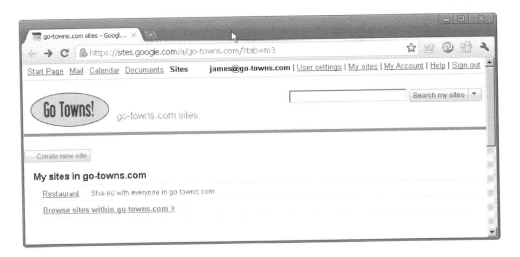

The initial screen shows only sites you have already created and the button to create another one. Click **Create new site** to get started to show the screen on the next page.

This page defines the basic attributes of your site. At a minimum, you must provide a site name of your choice. An address will be generated for you, although you can override what's suggested. All sites must follow the syntax of **http://sites.google.com/a/ yourdomain.com/yoursitename**.

Optionally, if you expand the **More Options** section, you can also add a brief site description to help visitors determine what the site is about, as well as categories. You also need to decide the site's visibility - you have three choices:

- **Private**: only the creator (you) and specified guests can view its content.

- **Everybody on your domain**: anyone who has Google Apps account on your domain can see the site.

- **Public**: the site is visible to anyone on the Internet, although public users cannot edit its content.

If you expand the **Choose a Theme** section, you can apply one of the many templates to your new site. Customization is fairly limited on Google Sites, but you can change the theme at any point in the future.

Finally, select a theme (which can be changed later if you don't want to choose now) and click **Create Site**. Congratulations, your Google Site is now live.

Using Site Templates

The blank template only creates one page - the home page - whereas a site template contains a range of pages most suitable for the project type selected. When you initially click **Create new site**, click **Browse the gallery for more** to see a complete list of public templates available:

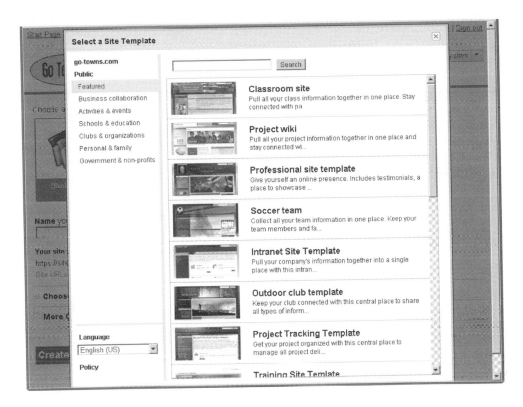

For example, clicking **Professional site template** creates a complete 12-page site together with pages specific for this kind of site. You can then edit each of these pages, replacing images and text, to make the look and feel your own.

The Basics

∙∙∙∙∙∙∙∙∙∙∙∙∙∙

Once your new site is created, the default view has four main sections:

1. **Header**: links to other Google services, sites, and help, followed by the Google Sites toolbar for managing the site.

2. **Navigation**: shows your site's page structure, together with the home page and sitemap (the only two you can see on a new site). The Edit Sidebar hyperlink only appears for user with administrative access.

3. **Current page**: this area shows the currently selected page, which is blank with a brand new site.

4. **Footer navigation**: every page has links to show recent activity, revision history, terms of service, report abuse, and an option to reformat to create a more print-friendly view. There is also an option to remove your access to the site in the event you hand over administration to another user.

    You can visit the Go Towns! Recipes site at https://sites.google. com/a/go-towns.com/recipes.

Creating pages

Click the **Create page** button from the main toolbar to open the new page screen:

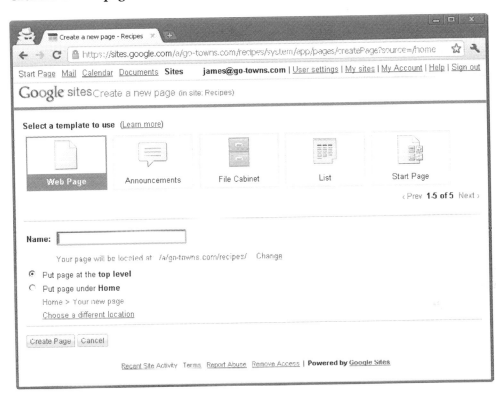

Enter a page name and choose a page type from the 5 options available:

- **Web page**: an unstructured page where you can enter text, images, tables, and embed spreadsheets, presentations, videos, and more.

- **Announcements**: designed for chronological information like news, status updates, blog posts, or notable events.

- **File Cabinet**: for managing documents relating to a page. Version history is automatically stored for documents (so you can revert to earlier versions).

- **List**: for lists of information, such as tasks, recipes, procedural steps, etc. You can choose from a list of templates or configure your own custom columns.

- **Dashboard**: a two-column webpage with four placeholder gadgets, designed for creating overviews or summaries.

Once the type is selected, you need to decide where in the site hierarchy the page will appear: at the top level, under the Home page, or in a different location. All pages must be discoverable within the site hierarchy (this differs from regular web sites which can have orphaned pages unlinked to the rest of the site).

The page hierarchy is more like a tree than the chapter structure of a book, and can run to multiple levels, like this:

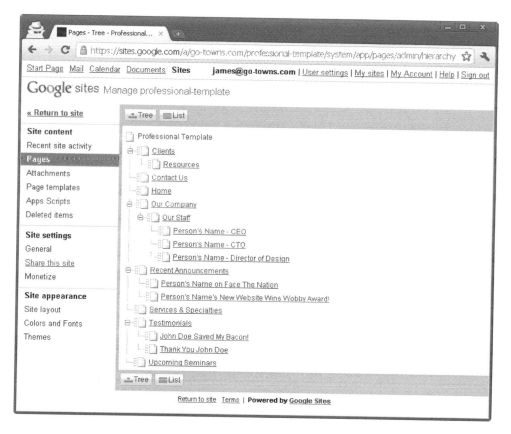

You can change the position of a page later, so for now just select the top level default. What happens next depends on the page type you have selected.

Webpage

The new page will open in the webpage editor. This WYSIWYG (what you see is what you get) editor is like a mini word processor that lets format your page, and creates the HTML in the background. The toolbar is actually almost identical to the one in the Google Docs word processor.

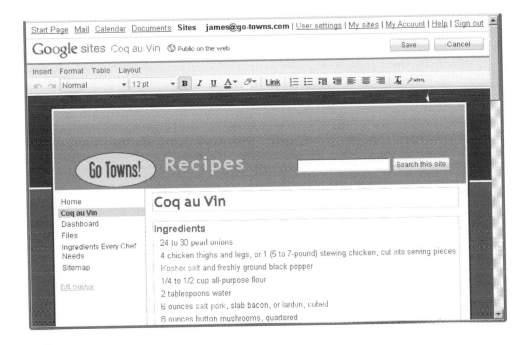

List type

Once you select a list type, Google will prompt you for a default type of list. You have a choice of three commonly used list templates, or you can create a new custom one from scratch (we'll review this in more detail in the next section).

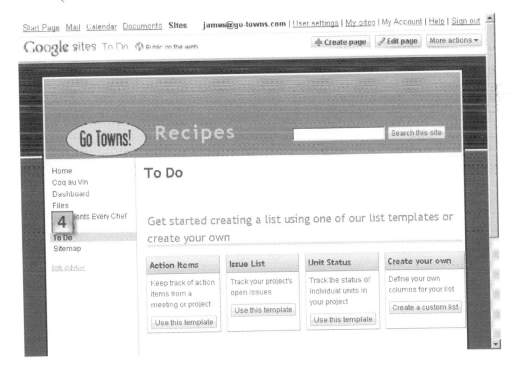

Dashboard type

The dashboard view shows four gadget-holders in two columns. Remember, gadgets are other services which extract data and create visual representations (customer lists on a map, sales on a chart, project progress on Gantt chart, Picasa web albums, etc.) You will also see the webpage editor container, since a dashboard is simply a webpage, and you can add text, images and other content around the gadgets.

File cabinet and announcement types both have simple initial pages, which we will cover more in the editing phase. To view this *Go Towns! Recipes* sample site, visit **https//sites.google.com/a/go-towns.com/recipes** or this book's web site.

Editing web pages

From the page creation option, you are automatically placed into the editing mode immediately after. If you want to edit a page otherwise, click the appropriate page in the left side navigation, and then click **Edit page**. You can only edit a page if you are the owner, or the owner has defined you as a contributor. As with everything in Google Apps, changes made are immediate. The exact editing screen you will see depends on the type of page.

Web pages and dashboards

The formatting toolbar in the main editor provides a range of basic formatting controls. Clicking a control will affect formatting from the current cursor position, or will apply the item to selected text.

Starting from left to right, here are the main controls, most of which you will have seen in other Google Apps applications:

- **Undo/Redo**: backtrack on changes, and reapply if needed.

- **Fonts/size**: limited to browser-friendly families of fonts and sizes.

- **Styles**: bold, italic, underline, foreground and background colors.

- **Hyperlink**: attach a URL to text (so it appears like this).

- **Numbering/bullets**: automatic numbering and indentation for lists.

- **Indentation controls**: change the left indent spacing of a paragraph.

- **Justification**: left, center and right justification.

- **Advanced**: remove all formatting and edit HTML directly.

The final option shows the editor contents with HTML markup. If you understand web design well, this mode is useful to see how the editor has translated the page, and also to make other design flourishes not available in the visual editor. It also means you can cut and paste from other HTML programs, which can save rebuilding pages from scratch. Google does not allow JavaScript, IFrames, CSS and other advanced features – these will be stripped out when you attempt to save.

Above the toolbar, the editor menus provide access to a range of other features:

- **Save/Cancel**: drafts are saved continuously, but only published when you hit the Save button. Cancel discards all changes.

- **Insert**: add media to your page, such as images, videos, Google documents and gadgets. We will look at this in more detail shortly.

- **Format**: apply heading styles to blocks of text, together with superscript, sub-script and strike-through.

231

- **Table**: insert tables into your page – these are intended for data display rather than layout control. Inserting and removing rows, columns and cells can also be performed from this menu.

- **Layout**: select up to three columns per page, with options to provide header and footer section or sidebars.

File cabinet

The file cabinet page is the simplest of the page types, and works as a storage device for your site. The range of allowable formats is more restrictive than Google Docs, and will fail to upload executable content (exe, dll, bat, etc.). You will receive an error if you try to upload an unapproved file type.

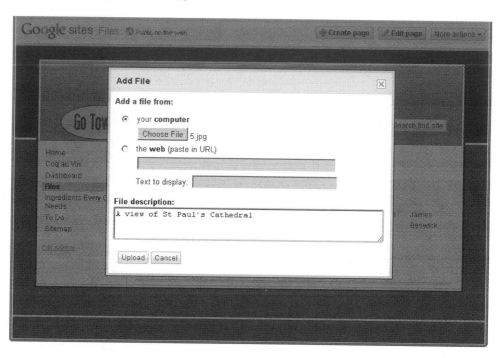

The main file cabinet options are:

- **Add file**: shows a dialog allowing you to select a file from your computer or from the Internet, together with an optional description.

- **Move to**: shows a list of defined folders for this page, with the option to create one. This is an organizational tool that allows files to be stored in named folders.

- **Delete**: permanently removes the file and all its version history.

- **Subscribe/unsubscribe from changes**: enables/disables real-time email notification when a file is added, updated or deleted.

From the main list, click the file name to download the latest copy or click the version number to see the revisions of the file. Uploading a file with the same name as an existing filename automatically creates a new version.

Announcements

Announcement pages are similar to web pages except that additional posts can be added by clicking **New Post**, much like the way a blog page works. The editor is the same as the webpage editor, but each post is called an announcement (read: blog post).

The only toolbar difference is a new button, called **Save Draft** so that posts can be created without being published (these drafts appear in the administrator's view of the page, but not the viewer's). As posts are added, they appear stacked in chronological order, most recent first, just like a blog.

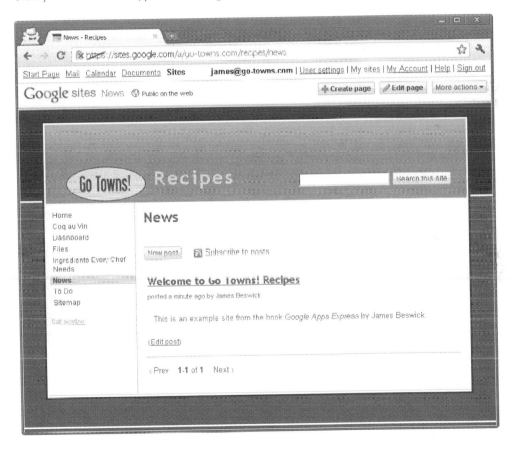

List type

The list type provides a way of tracking items in defined fields, similar to the way you might use an Access database table or Excel spreadsheet. This provides a structured way of describing the data needing for an item such as:

- An ingredient for a recipe.

- A period for a time tracking tool.

- A step in a project.

There are two types of editing here: customizing the fields for the item, and adding the actual items. Click **Customize** to define what constitutes an item and the following dialog appears:

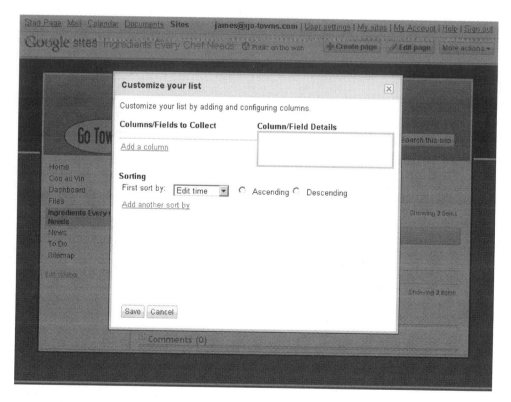

Click **Add a column** to show a new field called New Column with a default description on the right. You only need to define a description and a type.

There are five types available:

- **Checkbox**: the equivalent of a Yes/No or True/False entry.

- **Date**: for time-related fields.

- **Drop-down**: specify a range of acceptable entries for a field (e.g. day of week).

- **Text**: free-form text or numerical entries.

- **URL**: for web addresses and hyperlinks.

As you define each field, click **Add a column** to create new ones. You can then define the default sorting, which can be based upon one or more fields. Once you have finished, click **Save** to store the changes or **Cancel** to discard them.

Back on our *Go Towns! Recipes* website, we're using the list type for an ingredients list, where each field represents one of the possible field types.

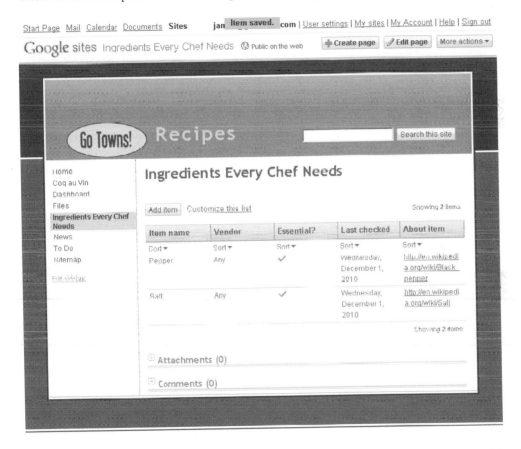

Once the list has been customized, adding items is the second step of editing. Click **Add item** to add to the list, or click an existing item to modify:

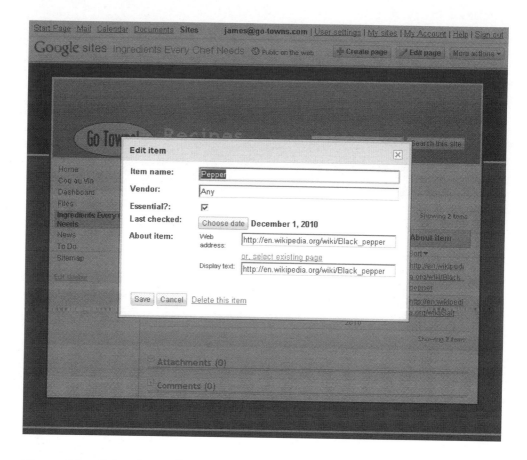

The resulting dialog shows all the fields you defined, with text, checkbox and drop-down controls where necessary. Date types have a calendar helper (click **Choose date** to view), and URLs provide two fields for the address and a display name.

More actions on pages

Viewing the page as somebody else

Since you are the administrator for your site, your view will be slightly different from other members (or the public view, if you opted for a publicly accessible site). If you want to see the page as everyone else sees it, click **More actions** ▶ **Preview page as viewer**. Alternatively, you can launch the URL in another browser where you are not signed in (e.g. use Internet Explorer instead of Mozilla Firefox), or simply sign out to achieve the same result.

Subscribing to changes

While the Wiki-culture is about empowering individual users to create and modify content, nevertheless it's still useful to know what's happening on your site. This is where subscriptions are useful, and on each page you can select **More actions ▶ Subscribe to changes** and receive an email when something happens.

If you want to know about changes site-wide, click **More actions ▶ Subscribe to site changes**, and Google will let you know when anything at all changes on the site. The natural trend in subscription monitoring is to listen to absolutely everything and then start unsubscribing as the site stabilizes (or your mailbox gets filled with notifications). Both options have the equivalent **Unsubscribe** features once a subscription is made.

Moving pages

Inevitably, pages do not always get created in the right place, or sometimes sites gets reorganized as they grow (current projects become completed projects, for example). Clicking **More Actions ▶ Move** enables you to see a new place for the current page. The Windows Explorer-style interface shows the hierarchy – click **Move** once you have found a new parent for the page.

Changing page settings

Each page is given a default range of settings when it is created, though there are times when you might want to fine-tune these. From the page you want to change, go to **More actions ▶ Page settings**.

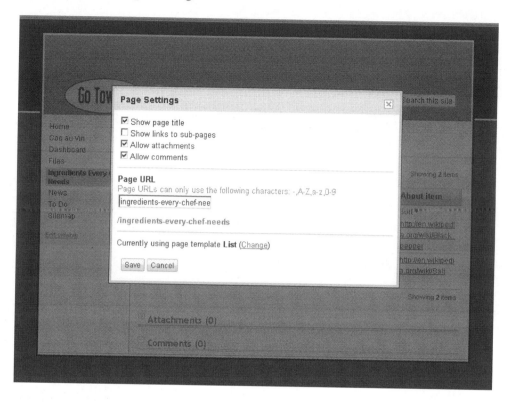

- **Show page title** places the page title at the top – once again, usually useful but not always, especially if the page uses large amounts of screen real estate or its purpose is obvious.

- **Show links to sub-pages** controls whether the sub-page list can be seen. This is a matter of personal preference but should usually be enabled to aid site navigation.

- **Allow attachments** and **Allow comments** enable or disable the collaborative elements of the page. The main reason to disable these is organizational – if your site is large and you want to centralize discussion and file storage, it makes sense to turn off these features on certain pages.

  If your site is publicly visible, anonymous users will not be able to comment or add an attachment, which helps reduce the amount of spam and irrelevant content. Contributors must be invited (and signed in) in order to leave comments or files.

Manage site options

Click **More Options** ▶ **Manage Site** to open the site management screen. There are three main categories tabs in this section.

Site content

- **Recent site activity:** Google Sites remembers all the activity that occurs on the site, viewable under this option. Click the **Subscribe** hyperlink to receive email notifications when activity occurs. It's not possible to delete individual entries on this page, but you can hide the recent activity page on your site from anonymous users in **Site settings** ▶ **General** ▶ **Access Settings**.

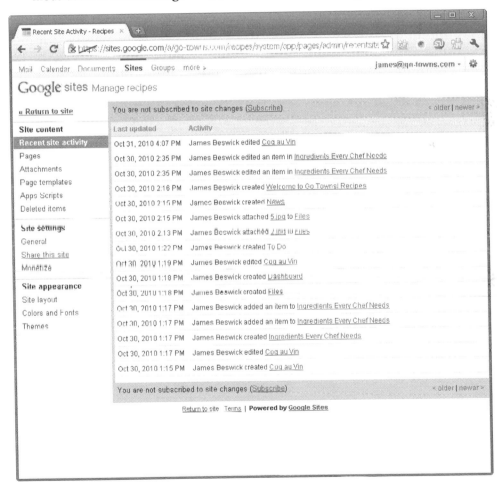

- **Pages** provides a list of all your site's pages and their hierarchy. You can view the pages in either a tree or list mode - the latter shows who created and last updated each page, with a list to all the page revisions.

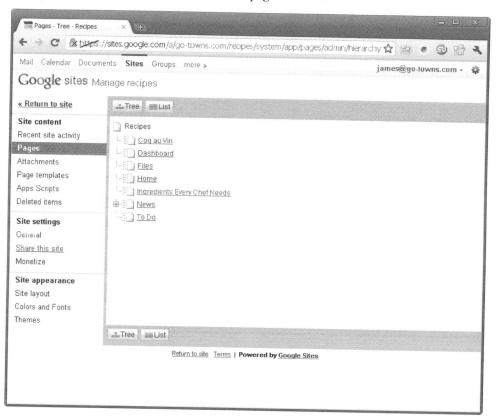

- **Attachments**: shows all side-wide file attachments together with their revisions and update statistics.

- **Page templates**: display the system-standard templates and any user-create templates for your Google Apps domain.

- **Apps Scripts**: although it's beyond the scope of this book, it's possible to develop your own JavaScript code to Google Sites. For more information on scripts, visit **http://code.google.com/googleapps/appsscript/guide_writing_scripts.html**.

- **Deleted items** is a site-wide recycle bin that you can use to rescue accidentally deleted items. Note that while individual files and pages can be restored, the Delete Site option will permanently remove everything.

Site Settings

Start Page Mail Calendar Documents **Sites**   james@go-towns.com | User settings | My sites | My Account | Help | Sign out

Google sites Manage recipes

« Return to site

Site content
Recent site activity
Pages
Attachments
Page templates
Apps Scripts
Deleted items

Site settings
General
Share this site
Monetize

Site appearance
Site layout
Colors and Fonts
Themes

Save changes Cancel

Site name
Recipes

☑ Show site name at top of pages

Site Category
food

Enter one or more comma-separated tags that others can use to find this
workspace (e.g. Business, Personal)

Site Description
A list of recipes provided by the fictional Go Towns! company.

Enter a short description that summarizes the purpose of this site.

Landing Page
[Home] Change
This is the default landing page that users will see when they visit your site:
(https://sites.google.com/a/go-towns.com/recipes/).

Statistics
☐ Enable Google Analytics for this site Learn more
Paste your Analytics Web Property ID here:

Example: UA-12345-12

Web Address Mapping
Map this Site See all Mappings
These links will only work correctly if you have enabled the next generation Control Panel.
Control Panel Settings

Google Webmaster Tools verification
Enter your Google Webmaster Tools meta tag verification below. Learn more

example: <meta name="google-site-verification"
content="RZWTXRO45nkPUX&2M6wpZ1sJ7_mwcy r5Wc_mwtus" />

Site display language
English (US)

Access Settings
Users who can access site activity: Anyone who can view this site

Users who can access revision history: Collaborators only

Site Actions
Copy this Site

Publish this site as a template

Delete this Site
WARNING: Deleting a site is permanent!
You'll be asked to confirm deletion before anything is erased.

Save changes Cancel

241

Click **Site Settings** ▶ **General** to view configuration options for your site:

- **Site name**: this is the main name for your site, and the checkbox below determines if the name appears at the top of every page.

- **Site category**: entering descriptive tags here will help others discover your site through Google Search.

- **Site description**: similarly, the description provides human-friendly information about the purpose of your site.

- **Landing page**: by default, visitors will arrive on the Home page from your main URL. Click **Change** to set another page as the site's entry point.

- **Statistics**: if you use Google Analytics, enter your unique web property ID in this box to enable data collection from your site.

- **Web address mapping**: this option allows you to set a top-level domain or sub-domain as your site address instead of the long-form URL. See chapter 2 for more details on CNAME mappings. Ideally, you should provide a mapping for every public site.

- **Google Webmaster tools verification**: GWT is an excellent free tool available to website owners that provide a wealth of useful information. You must confirm ownership of any new site registered with GWT by pasting the meta tag phrase here.

- **Site display language**: used to show the primary language of your site.

- **Access sites**: you can enable or disable both site activity and revision history for anonymous visitors here. However. collaborators can always view these pages.

- **Site Actions** ▶ **Copy this Site**: makes a duplicate of the existing site, with the option to include or exclude the original site's revisions and collaborators.

From: Site name   Recipes

To: Site name   [My new site]

          Your site will be located at this URL:
          https://sites.google.com/a/go-towns.com/ [my-new-site]
          Site URLs can only use the following characters: - ,A-Z,a-z,0-9

          ☑ Include Revisions
          ☑ Copy Site Members

[Copy site] [Cancel]

- **Site Actions ▶ Publish this site as a template**: you can publish a site as a template viewable by all members of your Google Apps account. This does make a site publicly viewable outside your domain. Once a site is published as a template, any changes are automatically published in the template gallery.

Make **Recipes** a template

About submitting a template

Site Template author:
- ⦿ James Beswick
- ○ james

When you submit a template to the go-towns.com gallery, anyone within go-towns.com will be able to use it by creating a copy of their own.

Site Template name:

By submitting a template, you agree to let anyone within go-towns.com use the content and styles that you created. Please make sure that you own the rights to distribute the content in your template.

Enter a description (max 500 characters)

After a template is submitted, any changes you make to it will show in the template gallery immediately. Please make changes with care!

Note: anyone in your domain will be able to view your template and any change you make to it.

Read more about templates

Template terms

Submit template   Cancel

- **Site Actions ▶ Delete this site**: this is self-explanatory, but be warned that it's a permanent step and an erased site is deleted forever.

Click on **Site settings ▶ Share this site** to open the familiar sharing dialog. As usual, you can define whether invitees can contribute and edit (collaborators) or have read-only access (viewers). Enter the range of email addresses and send invitations to have a defined group of people view the site, while it remains private to the rest of the world.

To make the site publicly visible, check the box next to Anyone in the world may view this site. While the site's content, files, comments and structure can be viewed by anyone (and will be indexed by Google just like a regular website), the public cannot contribute, comment or change anything. This limits the amount of spam that appears, but obviously means that unknown third parties have no way of interacting with you, unless you use the Forms tool (from Google Spreadsheets).

The next section down allows you to add Google AdSense on your site. Click on **Site settings ▶ Monetize** to start the process. You can use an existing AdSense account or create a new one, and choose to display the ads in the Site Sidebar or on widgets within individual pages.

Site Appearance

Click **Site appearance** ▶ **Site layout** ▶ **Change site layout**: to view the first group of options:

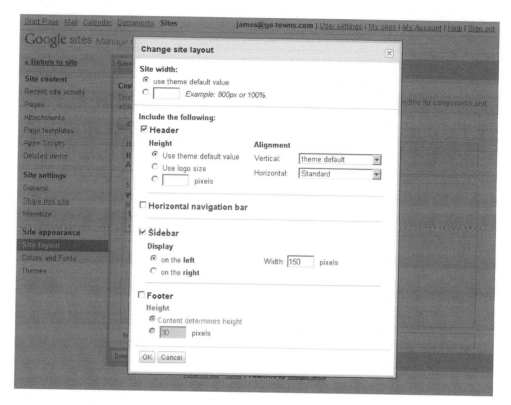

- **Site width**: new sites default to 100% of the browser width, but this can be changed to a smaller percentage or fixed pixel width.

- **Header**: can be toggled on and off, and you can set the height and alignment to match the current theme or have custom values.

- **Horizontal navigation bar**: this enables a bar just under the header that shows top-level pages on your site.

- **Sidebar**: can be positioned on the left or right of the main content with a specified width, or completely removed.

- **Footer**: provides the option to have an additional footer placed above the default system footer. This would typically be used for copyright notices, terms and conditions, privacy policies and so forth. You can also specify a height.

When you save any changes from the previous dialog, the layout will be updated in **Site appearance** ▶ **Site layout**.

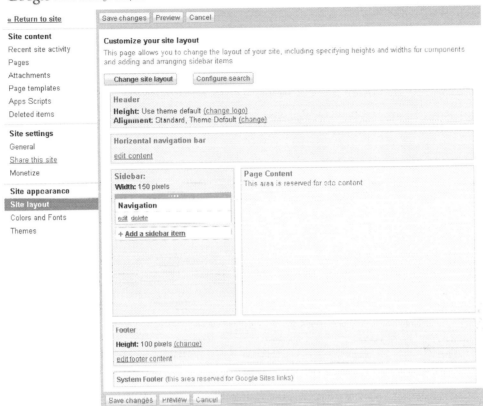

Back in the main Appearance configuration, you can define additional options:

- **Change logo** allows you to specify a graphic that appears in the header of every page - this can be unique to this site, or you can use the domain default logo.

- **Horizontal navigation preferences**: if you enabled this bar, you can specify which links are displayed, their order and formatting. Additionally, you can add URLs that are not part of your site structure.

- **Configure navigation**: specify how many pages deep will be displayed in the navigation, and if sitemap and recent site activity links are shown.

- **Add a sidebar item**: see below for other sidebar items available.

- **Edit footer content**: enables HTML editing of the optional second footer.

The **Preview** button gives an idea of what the specified layout will look like. Click **Save changes** to confirm the new settings, or **Cancel** to discard them.

Editing the sidebar

From the main view, there's an **Edit sidebar** link which will bring you to the same page. The idea of the sidebar is to provide an organizational hub for your site, and it consists of modules that provide different information to the user. By default, you are shown only the Navigation module, but there are several others you will see if you click **Add a sidebar** item:

- **AdSense**: places a Google AdSense unit in the sidebar - see the section on monetization in Site Settings earlier.

- **Text**: for arbitrary text items, which you can format using the web page editor.

- **Countdown**: provides a day countdown until a predefined event ("300 days until Thanksgiving") – once you specify the date, Google will dynamically calculate the number of days to display.

- **Recent site activity**: shows site-wide activity.

- **My recent activity**: as above, but filtered to show events for the current user.

You can add more than one of each type, which makes more sense for some items than others. Each item has individual settings which can be edited using the **Edit** hyperlink, and you can change the order of modules by dragging them around. Only an administrator can make sidebar modifications, so the layout appears fixed to other users.

Colors and Fonts

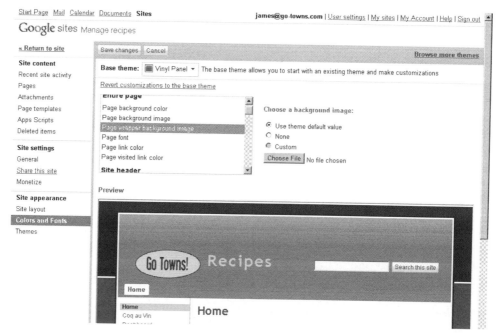

The second tab in the Site appearance section provides color and font control over a variety of page elements. These are all initially set by the theme you selected when you created the site.

While most elements simply involve selecting a color, others allow you to define a font, and a few allow images to be set. Images can be used to great effect to give your site a unique look, especially since they can be tiled (repeated) horizontally or vertically, so subtle gradients and patterns are easy to add.

Themes

The major difficulty with selecting colors all at once is that you need some design skill to pick a harmonizing set. If you're like me and colors aren't your strong point, themes are a big help here, since there are 23 preset color and image combinations that can be implemented instantly. Once you have selected a theme, you can still change individual parts the Colors and Fonts section.

Google Documents and Gadgets

In the webpage and dashboard editor, you can embed documents and gadgets. These extend the usefulness of your website, pushing it beyond static pages of information and repositories of data.

All the Google Documents you've read about in this book can be dropped into your sites pages, providing integrated views of information not directly in your site. Similarly, the gadgets can provide complex visualizations of your data that would usually require reasonable amounts of professional coding.

In our fictional recipes site, we could use Google Docs to:

- Plan a dinner, using an embedded Presentation slide show.

- Illustrate user feedback and ratings for recipes with Spreadsheets.

- Link to cookery articles in Google Docs.

- Show pictures from cooking competitions with Picasa albums.

- Show a schedule for upcoming events with Calendar.

- Collect user feedback with Forms.

Gadgets provide access to external services on your site, and there are a growing number available. By including gadgets on your site's pages, you are incorporating dynamic external data that makes your site more useful to your viewers and collaborators.

Building Gadgets into your pages.

From the webpage or dashboard editor, click **Insert ▶ More...** to see the entire library of gadgets available.

These are updated regularly, but here are highlights of the more useful ones:

- **Informational**: news, weather, stock quotes, clocks (including a world clock for multiple time zones) and driving directions.

- **Media**: MP3 players, Google Music and online TV channels.

- **Fun and games**: virtual aquariums, pac man, and cartoon strips.

- **Miscellaneous**: SMS messaging, calorie counters, and mashups.

A mashup is a collection of data and services combined to form some new view – such as weather forecasts in major cities shown on Virtual Earth, or house prices and crime statistics combined with USPS zip codes. Users can publish their mashups, and these become gadgets in Google Sites.

You can insert one or more gadgets into your site pages, with the aim of improving the user's experience. In the example below, Creative Cooking shows the weather in your region to help select a recipe, and allows visitors to send text messages to their dining guests. Both the weather and text messaging modules would be complicated pieces of software to develop from the ground up – gadgets provide a simple way for your site to consume these services quickly, and for free.

Don't forget, if you are a programmer (or have developers available), with a little JavaScript, HTML and XML you can build your own gadgets very quickly using the Google Gadget Editor. These work in most Google Applications and within any webpage as embedded objects. Searches in gadget libraries can generate significant traffic for their authors.

> For details on how to build gadgets, visit http://code.google.com/apis/gadgets.

Frequently Asked Questions

How do I set permissions for embedded Google Docs objects?

Embedding an object doesn't change the underlying access rights. If a user has access to the site but not the embedded Google Docs object, they will receive a warning to that effect. To fix this problem, change the permissions on the Google Docs object directly and it will propagate to the site automatically.

Can I add a custom favicon to my site?

A favicon - or favorite icon - is the custom logo that appears in a browser tab when you visit a site. To add one to your Google Site, simply go to **More actions ▶ Manage Sites ▶ Attachments** and upload a graphic with the name *favicon.ico*. For assistance in creating a favorite icon, visit **http://www.favicon.cc**.

Can I use any CSS with my site?

You cannot use global CSS for your site, but you can use inline styling. Although not every feature is supported, this can provide some additional flexibility in customizing your theme.

What are the limitations of Google Sites?

Although Google Sites is relatively flexible, there are some limitations which make it an inappropriate choice for some websites. Most importantly:

- Sites are limited to 100MB storage for free accounts and 10GB for Google Apps.

- Users are limited to the current themes and structure, with no arbitrary HTML or CSS allowed. Google Apps script can be used but JavaScript is disabled.

- Anonymous users may view a site but cannot add comments or make changes. This is different to many CMS-driven sites that allow anonymous comments.

Google also has specific rules regarding specific types of content (i.e. sexually explicit material, affiliate promotions, spam, impersonation, etc.) and will disable any site that violates their terms and conditions. Most organizations shouldn't have a problem, but if you have questionable content, you should choose an alternative platform.

If your site is disabled and you don't believe you violate their content rules, submit a request for a review at **http://www.google.com/support/sites/bin/request. py?contact_type=disabled**.

11394230R0015

Made in the USA
Lexington, KY
01 October 2011